Animal
and Plant
Life Spans

From infancy through maturity to death may be a life span of 39 or more years for these chimpanzees—far more than a shrew's maximum of two years and modest compared to the 150 years that a large tortoise may live.

Animal and Plant Life Spans

ALICE L. HOPF

Holiday House · New York

Library of Congress Cataloging in Publication Data

Hopf, Alice Lightner, 1904–
  Animal and plant life spans.

  Includes index.
  SUMMARY: Explores the influence of heredity,
behavior, and environment on the life span of animals
and plants.
  1. Longevity—Juvenile literature. [1. Longevity]
I. Title.
QH528.5.H66   574.3′74   77-17571
ISBN 0–8234–0320–3

For my brother Clarence,
doctor and scientist

Contents

Smaller dogs, such as the cocker spaniel at the left, seem to live longer, on the whole, than big dogs such as the boxer, right.

1

Every Dog Has Its Day

If you were lucky enough to be given a dog when you were a small child, you enjoyed the companionship of this "best friend" while you were growing from childhood to maturity. Yet by the time you were 15 years old, and looking forward to becoming a young adult, your pet was an old dog, or very probably dead. This is a law of life, but one that is hard to take when we see the dog that romped with us through childhood now unable to follow us to the woods or to enjoy a long walk in the city. Instead, he is limping and maybe yelping with pain, perhaps blind and deaf, so that we have to make the unhappy decision of putting him permanently to sleep, while we ourselves are only approaching our best years of strength and activity.

Why is this? It seems unfair and unequal. But the fact is that every creature, every form of life on earth, has its own built-in life span. Every animal faces a variety of hazards as it goes through life. It may be eaten by a predator. It may be killed by some accident or become a victim of a disease. But if it manages to escape all these perils and live longer than most, it will eventually come to the end of its life span. And that span has a different length for all living things.

It used to be said that one year of a dog's life is equal to seven years of a human's. But it is not quite that simple. For one thing, different species of dogs have a different life expectancy. Oddly enough, the smaller breeds seem to live longer than the larger ones. Records for cocker spaniels and Pekingese show some of them living to be 13 to 15 years old. But large English mastiffs seldom live longer than nine years. Dogs that are able to live into the teens are usually medium-sized mongrels.

In this century, scientists have begun to make a serious study of the differing life spans of animals and other forms of life. For if we can find out what it is that makes one animal live longer than another, we may be able to help people to live longer, healthier lives. The eminent scientist Dr. Alex Comfort, in his book *Ageing: The Biology of Senescence*, gives many useful tables of age records of all kinds of animals. His detailed discussion covers the various orders of the animal world, and his tables and records have been chiefly followed in this book.

At first, in the new research, a lot of myths and misinformation had to be weeded out, for until the present century, exact records were hardly existent. People would say, "Oh, that parrot is hundreds of years old!" But there would be no records to prove it. Hearsay is usually faulty. Similarly, until birth registration was established in the late nineteenth century, there was no proof of the exact age of a person. When scientists began to investigate claims of extreme old age, they found that most of them were exaggerated. In one case, the same cottage had been occupied by three generations, father, son, and grandson, all having the same name. Thus their combined years had been credited to one individual.

What Makes a Long Life?

But what is it that makes one species, or one individual within a species, live longer than the rest? This question is still being studied by experts in many fields of science. At first glance it might seem to be size that has something to do with it. Some insects live rather brief lives. The monarch butterfly lives about eight or nine months, migrating with the seasons from north to south. Aphids, after over-wintering in the egg, live only a few weeks in the summer, having a total life span of about a year. The smaller animals, such as rats and mice, live much shorter lives than do the larger ones. Among the domestic animals, horses live longer than dogs and cats. But it is soon apparent that size cannot be the criterion for longevity. Domestic cats have a longer life span than dogs. And we have already noted that the bigger dogs do not live as long as the smaller ones. So what else might be the answer?

Some investigators have suggested that the relationship of body weight to heartbeat may have a bearing. Or that the relationship of brain weight to body size may be the clue. Thus, the raccoon, having a relatively large brain, can live to be 14 years old. But the opossum, which is almost the same size as the raccoon but has a much smaller brain, lives for only seven years.

David P. Willoughby, writing in *Natural History,* has considered the ages at which certain animals mature (generally defined as the age at which they can repro-

In their lives of less than a year, monarch butterflies travel thousands of miles. Here they cluster by the hundreds, resting on their migration south for the winter.

duce). A dog becomes mature at one and a half years. But if one multiplies this by seven, one gets 10.5 years for a human. And a child in temperate zones does not usually mature till about 13 (though in hot countries it may be nine or ten). So the seven-year theory is not very sound, and depends on various ifs and buts.

Willoughby gives a formula for estimating the maximum age of any species of mammal. The factors he works with represent the average age at maturity, the average age at death, and the potential maximum age for the species. Using this method, he finds that a dog of 28 years (which would be extremely rare), a cat of 32 years, and a horse of 38 years are all about equal to a human of 102 years.

The twentieth century brought in the study of cells and hormones, and in recent years research has concentrated on these as the probable controls for the life span. In the insects, a hormone known as the juvenile hormone has been found to trigger the changes in growth that bring the insect through the several stages from egg to adult.

There is a certain difference between the cells that make up animal life and those found in plants. Animal cells are covered with a soft membrane, whereas plant cells are encased in a relatively rigid membrane. In the animal kingdom there are two general types of cells: those that are continually dividing and making new cells (as in the skin) and those that rarely divide or renew themselves (as in brain or muscle). In addition, the body contains some noncellular material, such as collagen. It is possible that this is not renewed as the animal grows older.

Each cell contains within it a chemical called DNA.

This is the substance that holds the code of life. It regulates the genes so that each cell divides or operates in the proper way. When an animal has lived for a certain span of time, the cells that divide and restore themselves may cease to do so. The cells that do not divide may be lost or damaged. The results are what we know as aging.

How Cells Are Injured

Cells can be damaged or killed in a number of ways. Radiation can kill them or damage the vital DNA within them. With cells that divide and increase, this damage can be surmounted. But with cells that never divide or replace themselves, the injury is permanent. Thus, aging often shows up first in the muscles or the brain or liver, where fresh cells do not substitute for old ones.

Since the invention of the atomic bomb and the tragedies of Hiroshima and Nagasaki, we have all become aware of the lethal effects of ionizing radiation, such as X-rays and gamma rays. Scientists are still busy investigating these effects. One of the first to do so was Dr. Howard Curtis of Brookhaven National Laboratory in Long Island, N.Y., who treated mice with radiation. He found that while the mice died of the same diseases as did nonradiated mice, they grew old quickly and died much earlier. But while we are all aware of the harmful effects of radiation created by humans and try to control it, we have always been constantly exposed to radiation originating in rocks and coming from the cosmic rays of outer space. This natural radiation is always chipping away at the health of our cells.

Muscle cells, shown here, do not replace themselves, so aging becomes apparent earlier in muscles than in skin, for example, which constanly grows new cells as old ones die off.

Other causes of cell damage are the pollution in our water and atmosphere and the many chemicals and preservatives added to the food we eat. Even such things as coffee may contribute damage to the cells, and alchohol is considered by physiologists to be a slow poison, though not many laymen think of it in those terms.

But why should this aging process appear earlier in some species than in others? Why should some individuals begin to become decrepit sooner than others of the same species? Some scientists have guessed that every individual carries within it a "biological time clock" that after a certain period cuts off the life processes and brings living to an end.

The Remarkable Glands

In the search for this mysterious clock, scientists have begun to investigate the hormones. These are substances released throughout the body by various glands. The remarkable effects that the glands and their hormones have on the human body have been known and studied for a fairly long time. Perhaps the control that the juvenile hormone exerts in the development of insects has encouraged scientists to look into this aspect of aging.

Glands can make one tall or short, thin or fat. They control the beating of the heart and the workings of the liver, kidneys, and digestion. They determine when a boy or girl becomes mature and they have a bearing on the development of personality. So it may well be that they determine how long we live.

It is well known that women on the whole live longer than men. This is generally ascribed to the effects of the female hormone, estrogen. But more recently some researchers have begun to suspect that this is not the case. In men, it may be some harmful effect of the male hormone (testosterone) which shortens the life span. This theory seems more believable since it has been found that castrated males are likely to live longer than normal males.

In earlier times, the operation to remove the male sex glands was performed on young singers who wished to retain their high, boyish voices; or the men picked to guard the harems of eastern potentates, who after the operation were known as eunuchs. Today it is chiefly performed on mentally retarded or psychotic males. When scientists made a study of such individuals in institutions, it was found that the average life span for normal males was 55.7 years. But for eunuchs it was 69.3 years.

There are many other glands in the body besides the sex glands. The largest is the pancreas, which weighs less than three ounces. The smallest is the pineal, the size of a grape seed. Then there are the thyroid, the four parathyroids, the two adrenals, the pituitary, and the thymus. Altogether, the glands may weigh between four and seven ounces, yet they influence the size and shape, the functioning, and the personality of the individual. One or more of them may determine how long that individual will live.

For a long time it was believed that the pituitary gland was the "master" that controlled the proper functioning of the body. It has been found to regulate the other endocrine glands, to stimulate or depress them. But more recently it has been discovered that the pituitary itself is regulated by the hypothalamus, a control center in the brain. Perhaps the process of aging is governed there, for the pituitary in turn influences the thyroid and adrenal glands to release their hormones and control the various functions of the body.

Today, attention has turned to the pineal and the thymus glands. The pineal is a small bulge of brain located between the two hemispheres. (All mammalian brains are separated into two parts.) In the young, the pineal appears to be a gland, but in older people it becomes hard. It used to be considered something left over in the body from earlier evolution, like the appendix. But now scientists are beginning to suspect that it may be connected to the biological clock which regulates the aging process.

Such a clock must be responsible for the maturing of the young at puberty.

An example of a biological clock has been observed in rats. It has a rhythm of about 24 hours and controls the amount of serotonin in the rat's pineal gland. At midnight this is very low and by noon it has risen to three times that low amount. The cycle continues to repeat every 24 hours, but it has no relation to day and night, light or dark. It is a true biological clock that keeps going in the same way even if the rats are kept in total darkness.

Another instance of a biological clock appears in bamboo trees. One species of bamboo that grows in China, with the scientific name of *Phyllostachys bambusoides,* blooms once about every 120 years. There is an ancient Chinese record of its blooming in the year 919 A.D., and since then, with remarkable regularity, it has flowered and produced seeds approximately every 120 years. Over the centuries, these bamboos have been transplanted to many countries, where they must adjust to different weather and soil conditions. But whether the trees are growing in Russia, Japan, England, or America, they all flower and set seeds at about the same time intervals, 120 years. Their biological clocks continue to work from some internal power.

Perhaps the pineal gland in humans has some similar clocklike function. Work on this theory has only recently begun, so as yet we do not know.

The thymus gland is another mysterious organ. Little was known about it until 1961, when an English doctor removed the thymus from infant mice and found that they soon sickened and died. Some experts now believe that the thymus regulates the body's immune system and thus may control diseases like cancer and arthritis. At the present time, hormones are believed to have more bearing on the aging process than any other thing in the body, and work is being done on the problem in laboratories all over the world.

Animals and Their Ages

Of all the mammals, humans live the longest. But to do research and observation on our own species is difficult. The observer may not live much longer than his subject. Most of the information must be acquired from birth registrations, insurance records, and such. Work in the laboratory must be done on creatures like rats and mice, rabbits, and even fruit flies, where the generations move quickly past the observer and into his records.

But observing animals in the laboratory or in zoos, or domestic animals, may give false answers, for they are not in their natural habitat. And captive animals do not usually keep in top physical condition as do those in the wild. On the other hand, few wild animals live out their lives to the maximum. Old age is seldom observed among them. There are too many hazards: floods, famine, predators, and disease. Survival is a chancy thing and even the strongest and most sagacious is apt to succumb before its period has run out. Sir Francis Bacon, writing in the sixteenth century in his *Historia Vitae et Mortis,* said, "in household beasts the idle life corrupts; in wild, the violence of the climate cuts them off."

Early in this century, an English scientist, S. S. Flower,

collected information on the life spans of animals. Over many years he added to his list, but unfortunately he died before he could complete it. However, he left a wealth of carefully verified material for later students and he was able to correct many of the unsubstantiated claims for such creatures as elephants and parrots.

In many animals, age can be estimated by their horns, teeth, or scales (in fish). These are structures that grow yearly in a regular pattern and can be counted, as tree rings are counted to learn the age of a tree. In this way, the teeth of seals can be used by counting the layers of cementum, a bony layer in the gum. The horns of sheep and goats and the antlers of caribou have rings or similar growth that can be counted, and whales have plugs of ear wax that indicate their age.

Birds are more difficult. Only the lyrebird, it seems, has progressive changes in its feathers that betray its age. But reptile ages can now be determined by growth zones in their bones. Even in fossil Australian lizards this information can be read from the bones, which like tree rings, also give indications of weather cycles during the animal's lifetime.

The only mammal that approaches humans in length of life is the elephant. It can live to be 60 years old and some individuals may live past 70. To find creatures that outstrip us in longevity, we must go to the reptiles. Many species of land tortoise have been known to live well past 100; even up to 150 in at least one well authenticated case.

Birds used to be thought of as very long-lived. But compared to the tortoises, their accomplishments in lon-

It is not always possible to tell animal ages; the lyrebird, above, is one of the very few bird species that show age by feather changes. Reptiles, such as the young snapping turtle below, show ages by specific changes in bone growth.

gevity are rather modest. An eagle owl (*Bubo bubo*) has been proved to have lived for 68 years and greater sulphur-crested cockatoos (*Kakatoë galerita*) have been reported at 69, 80, and 120 years.

Toads, frogs, and salamanders seem like small creatures that would hardly live more than a few years. But our well known bullfrog (*Rana catesbiana*) has been recorded at 15 years and one of the tree frogs (*Hyla coerulea*) at 16. It is true that most of these figures are for captive animals, which lead a protected existence in the zoo or the laboratory. The bullfrog listed above was a captive. Its wild relatives are credited with only 8 to 10 years. But with so many birds and animals (including humans) looking for a taste of frogs' legs, this is hardly extraordinary. And in recent years so many frogs have been caught for use in the biology classroom and laboratory that there is some fear that the species most used, *Rana pipiens*, may become extinct.

In fish the life expectancy does seem to run to size. The colorful little tropical fish, much prized for the aquarium, seldom live more than a year or two. Swordtails are listed at two to three years and the others are much the same. Possibly they do better in the wild, but nobody knows. The European river catfish (*Silurus glanis*), on the other hand, which weighs up to 181.5 kilograms (about 400 pounds), has been known to live for over 60 years. A beluga sturgeon, 424 centimeters long (almost 14 feet) and weighing over 1 metric ton (2204.6 pounds), was aged at 75 years by scale count. Similarly, a halibut three meters (about 10 feet) long was found to be over 60. Between these two extremes, we find that a pike weighing

15.5 kilograms (about 34 pounds) turned out to be 13 to 14 years old.

The ancient Romans kept fish ponds where they raised fresh fish for the table, and they have left records of their interest in the ages of their captives. Some moray eels, then considered a delicacy, were known to be over 60 years old. The famous orator Crassus even mourned a particular eel when it died.

The Spineless Ones

All these creatures are what we call vertebrates, or animals with backbones. But there are many classes of animals (invertebrates) that do not have backbones. These include the insects and many of the creatures of the sea. Most insects are short-lived by our standards, so one would perhaps hardly expect invertebrates in general to have a long life. But many sea invertebrates have an astonishing span. For example, one sea anemone (Actinia) collected by a British naturalist in 1828 died in 1887 at an estimated age of 66 years.

The crayfish appears to have a life span of 15 to 30 years, and such creatures as clams can live to a remarkable age. Some species live only a few months to a few years, yet the age of others has been found to be in the 50's and even at the 70-80-year level.

As just noted, some insects have short lives, living about a year. Beetles do better, living in the adult stage, according to the species, anywhere from three to ten years. Among the social insects, which includes the bees and ants, it is the female (or queen) that is long-lived.

During the busy summer months, the hard-laboring worker bees are worn to death in a few weeks. But the queen bee can live for years, producing eggs all summer and hibernating with her hive during the cold months. Some ant queens have been aged at 15 years.

Some spiders are also remarkably long-lived. Many females can live from 7 to 11 years, and the large American tarantulas have been known to live up to 20 years.

The really ancient forms of life on this planet are trees. Some of them are so old that it is hard to imagine their ages; their life spans go back to the beginnings of history. People have always held great trees in awe and endowed them with supernatural powers or godlike spirits. Myths and legends cling to them, and in many cases their age has been exaggerated, as though we humans like to make a good thing better. Thus many a churchyard yew tree has been credited with some 6000 years. But when scientists began to investigate the matter, they found that a mere 1000 years was probably the limit.

Still, there are other trees that live even longer and are well worth some attention. The macrozamia trees in Australia, the redwoods and sequoias of California, the bristlecone pines, and the famous tule cypress in Mexico are a few.

2

Animals
Without
Spinal Columns

The Water Bears

Strangely enough, some of the very smallest creatures, almost invisible to the naked eye, have developed a way of extending their lives to extraordinary lengths. They are often called water bears. These little creatures live almost everywhere: in fresh water, in salt water, and in the soil, and they are found everywhere from the Arctic to the Antarctic, from ocean depths to the highest mountains. More than 400 species have been described, and they range in size from one-tenth of a millimeter to one millimeter (about ⅕₅ of an inch). They must be observed and studied under the microscope.

Various microscopic animals were first seen by a pioneer microscopist, the Dutch scientist Anton van Leeuwenhoek, in the seventeenth century. He startled the scientific world when he began describing the amazing life that his lenses showed him in a drop of water. Much later, in 1773, a German scientist named Johann Goeze described what he called "a little water bear." Three years later the great Italian naturalist Lazzaro Spallanzani called this creature *il tardigrado,* "the slow stepper." From this has come their scientific name, tardigrades. But many people still refer to the animals as water bears, because their four pairs of legs have little bearlike claws and they move in a slow, lumbering manner.

The remarkable thing about water bears, as well as some other microscopic animals, is their ability to survive extreme changes in their environment by seeming to dry up and die, only to come to life again when moistened. The early observers were fascinated by this discovery and considered it a true case of revival from death. But more recent students, hoping to get away from any suggestion of the supernatural, now call the phenomenon suspended animation or, to use the strictly scientific term, crypto-biosis.

The water bear has a stout body covered with cuticle. Sometimes this is smooth and thin. But some have all kinds of "decorations" on their bodies: plates reminiscent of a rhinoceros or a dinosaur, pores, spines, and filaments, some of which may be used for sensing and feeling. The cuticle slows the loss of water from evaporation. The animals come in a variety of colors: red, yellow, gray, pink, purple, green, and even white. This often depends on what they have been eating, as the color of the food tends to color the animal. They are also equipped with a pair of piercing stylets and a mouth tube, with which they pierce the cell walls of plants or the bodies of other animals and then feed by sucking out the juices.

The salt-water species live between grains of sand or on seaweeds or other algae floating in the water. They feed on plant or animal life at the surface of the sea and are them-

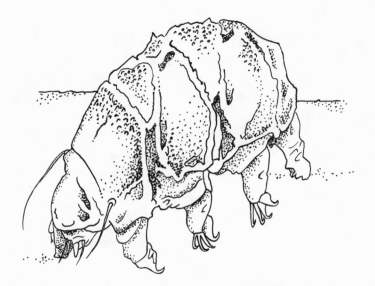

When it is enlarged about 800 times, a tardigrade suggests some monster from the prehistoric past. Its rugged cuticle helps it to retain water during its long "dead" periods.

selves eaten by larger creatures. The fresh-water species can be found in mosses, pond plants, and the mud of ponds, puddles, streams, and lakes. The earth-dwelling tardigrades live in mosses, lichens, leaf litter, and just plain soil.

Tardigrades have two separate sexes—something not always true of the lower animals. But in a few species there are no males, and the females reproduce by parthenogenesis, birth of infants from unfertilized eggs. If the tardigrade is one of the species living in water, the male may deposit his sperm in the old cuticle that the female has just shed during molting. Then the female will deposit her eggs there. But in land-living species, the male usually injects his sperm into the female. The female then lays her eggs, sometimes in her molted cuticle, sometimes attached to something in the environment. The eggs themselves often have projections of various sorts, which may be a protection against predators. Or they may be covered with pores. The eggs hatch after two weeks and the animals then go through two or three molts in the process of growing. After that they become adult tardigrades, ready to mate and produce eggs.

Years of Dryness

The usual life span of the water bear is less than a year, but with its remarkable ability for suspended animation, it can extend that period to 100 years or more. Some dried moss that had been kept in a museum for 120 years was moistened and brought forth living tardigrades. How does the water bear do this? Scientists are still studying the animals to find out more of their secrets, which may lead to a better understanding of the aging process in higher animals—including humans.

Suspended animation occurs normally in water bears as a result of changes in their environment. In the great variety of conditions under which they live, there are weather changes—too hot, too cold, high winds, or drying-out of the atmosphere. This can lead to lethal situations for these very small creatures. The pond in which they are living may completely dry up, bringing death to fish and other water creatures. Eighty-five per cent of the tardigrade's body is water, and this is lost gradually until only 3 per cent of the water is left. The animal stops moving and contracts into a barrel-shaped form, called a "tun" by the scientists. In this form, the water loss proceeds gradually. In nature, any rapid loss of water can kill, but this gradual loss seems to be one of the keys to the tardigrade's suspension of active life.

Water bears also go into suspended animation when temperatures go below freezing or when the oxygen content of their environment gets too low. In laboratory studies they have been found to survive in a vacuum (which may make them eligible for space experiments) and to withstand unusual amounts of X-ray radiation.

This unique ability to survive extreme conditions may be responsible for the water bear's worldwide distribution. It is believed that they are dispersed principally by the wind. But also rainwater, ocean waves and currents, as well as other creatures such as insects and birds, have carried them to distant regions. However far they may travel during suspended animation, they need only wait for better environmental conditions to arrive before reviving and resuming their life activities.

Insects

How does one recognize an insect? That's fairly easy, if it's an adult. In that case, it will have three parts to its body (head, thorax, and abdomen), and three pairs of legs. The young, usually called nymphs if they look like their parents, or larvae if they don't, are harder to recognize. In the more advanced species, they look entirely different from their parents. Who could imagine that the crawling, leaf-chewing caterpillar would grow to be the

An insect, unlike spiders and other arachnids, has just six legs, and a quite separate head, thorax, and abdomen.

winged, nectar-sipping butterfly? This astonishing change is called metamorphosis and is one of the wonders of the animal world.

All insects start life as an egg, from which a small nymph or larva hatches, to begin eating its way to maturity. As it eats it grows bigger, and when it becomes too big for its integument ("skin")—which is what holds the insect together, since it has no backbone—it rests and then sheds the integument. Underneath is a new and larger covering, wrinkled, which allows it to fit inside the old one. The insect swallows air or water, thus inflating itself and stretching out the wrinkles; and it stays blown up till the new skin hardens. Then it grows until this skin also becomes too small. After it has passed through several of these larval stages, it is ready for the transformation into an adult. In the simpler forms of insects this is achieved by one final molt. The grasshopper, for instance, acquires its flying wings at this point. But for the more advanced forms of insects—such as the butterflies and moths, beetles, bees, and wasps—there is a third form, the pupa, which the creature must assume before becoming an adult.

This is the complicated life cycle of such insects: egg, larva, pupa, and adult. Scientists have been studying it for many years and have found that it is controlled by hormones. There are believed to be three types of hormones involved: the brain hormone, the molting and growth hormones, and the juvenile hormones. It is thought that after hatching from the egg, the insect's brain hormone sends a signal to the growth and juvenile hormones. They enable the insect to grow and molt and then become even bigger. When it has reached the proper size, the juvenile hormone is turned off and the larva goes into pupation. The molting hormone, however, continues to function and brings the insect through the pupal stage, in which it transforms into an adult. During this period, all hormones may cease to function if the insect is to hibernate as a pupa. Finally, when spring has come, the brain hormone goes to work again and starts the growth hormone. But not the juvenile hormone, which is no longer needed for the adult insect. The creature sheds its skin for the last time and emerges as an adult. Perhaps this turning on and off of hormones in insects is similar to functions in the higher animals that control their growth and aging.

The Vinegar Fly

An insect with a very short life span is the vinegar fly (*Drosophila melanogaster*). People often call it the fruit fly. These are tiny flies that are more of a personal nuisance than a destructive pest. In summer they may be seen in swarms around ripe fruit in markets or even at the dinner table.

Here is one case where the smallness of the animal corresponds with the shortness of its life span, for in a warm summer they can complete their entire life cycle within 10 days. For this reason they have been very useful to science; results of breeding experiments appear in a short time. They are now famous as the tool used by the geneticist Thomas Hunt Morgan when he was verifying Mendel's laws of heredity. Drosophila also has very large chromosomes—the structures that carry genes—in the cells of the salivary glands, making it easier for scientists to count them. Morgan crossed flies that had red eyes with those that had white eyes and noted the percentages of each color in the offspring. He also worked with gray and yellow body colorings. With the short life span, he could make many crossings in a short period of time. His work began in the early 1900s and by 1926 he had learned enough to publish a book, *The Theory of the Gene,* which was the beginning of the great revolution in genetics, still going on today, and now developing into the

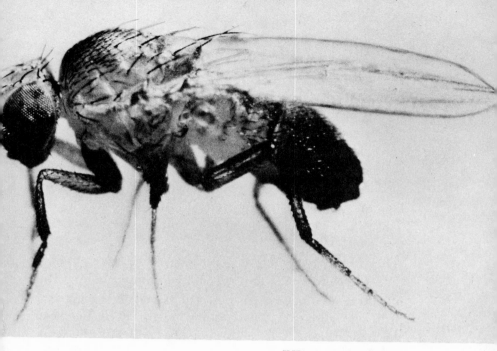

The vinegar fly's short life span is a great advantage to studying genetics; within ten days or so a biologist can see the results of his breeding experiments.

new science of genetic engineering.

Vinegar flies lay their eggs in garbage pails and on rotting fruit lying on the ground. The tiny larvae are whitish and they stay in the decaying fruit or vegetation. They eat yeasts and other fungi and make their way to the outside of the semiliquid mass to find a dry spot where they can pupate. At the front end of the pupal shell is a pair of short horns through which the creature breathes.

These flies are still being used in laboratories for research purposes, and now that science has turned its attention in a big way to animal behavior, that study has not been overlooked. One group at Columbia University studied the mating behavior of *Drosophila paulistorum,* a species of fly from Brazil. Dr. Lee Ehrman has described what she calls the four elements of courtship.

At first the male approaches the female and runs around her. He never completes the circle, but changes direction every 330 degrees. Soon he begins to tap the legs and abdomen of the female, touching her lightly. This gentle contact seems to assure him—in some sense of the word—that this is a female and one of the right species. In between tappings, he does some more circling.

In the third stage, the male places himself behind the female in a crouching position. He extends one wing and begins to vibrate it. While doing this, he taps and licks the female. Finally he makes a rush, and using the wing that had been vibrating, he pushes himself up onto the female and mating takes place. The female slightly spreads her wings and the male rests his forelegs upon them, thus being helped to keep his balance during the 17 minutes that mating continues. Meanwhile, the female may walk about, sometimes even being followed by other males. At last she gets rid of the male by kicking him, folding in her wings, and tossing her body about.

Largely because of their very short life span, these little insects have been helpful in extending our knowledge in many fields of science.

The Shiny-Winged Ones

One group of insects, known as the hymenoptera, may have in some cases extended the life span by developing a social way of life. These are primarily the bees, ants, and wasps; they have glossy membranous wings with simple patterns of veins. Many of the species in this order still live solitary lives, and in these cases the life cycle usually corresponds with the yearly change of seasons. The life span of individuals rarely exceeds one year.

But with the bees and ants this has been greatly extended. These insects build large nests, often compared to human cities. With this protection against the hazards of the environment, they have been able in some cases to greatly extend their life span.

The honeybee, probably the best known bee species, is not native to the Americas. Instead we had the bumblebee, an industrious pollinator, but one that has not developed its social life as highly as the honeybee. Thus the colony of bumblebees dies every winter. Only the young, fertilized females survive to build a new colony the following spring. The honeybees, which were imported from Europe about 300 years ago, have lived as domestics with humans for 4000 years, building their colonies in the various hives that we supply for them. They get along equally well in the wild, where they occupy hollow trees or similar shelters.

There are three castes of bees: the workers, infertile females which are seen busily gathering honey from flowers; the drones, which are the males and appear only when needed to mate with a queen; and the queen bee, a fertile female which lays the tens of thousands of eggs that, once hatched, populate the colony. There is only one queen to a hive; and while the life of a worker in midsummer may be only a few weeks, the queen can live as long as seven years.

Ants are even longer-lived than bees. They too have de-

A worker honeybee, seen here on an alfalfa blossom, lives only a few weeks during its busy midsummer season.

veloped the caste system. The great majority are infertile females, known as workers. Some of them have especially strong jaws or large heads, fitting them for work as soldiers (the ant city must be protected from raiding ants) or doors (the head fits exactly into the entrance hole to the nest). There are also the fertile females, or queens, that lay all the eggs. Males, sometimes called kings, appear when needed to fertilize the new queens, and then die. Unlike the bees, ants sometimes have more than one queen in a colony.

Ants have extended their life span even farther than have bees. A worker of *Formica fusca* may live for seven years. And the queen has been known to live more than ten years. Another species, *Lasius niger*, has a queen that may live for 19 years.

The Periodical Cicada

Perhaps the longest-lived insect in the world is the periodical cicada. There are cicadas all over the world, but we want to look here at the several species that are popularly known as "17-year locusts." They are found only within the United States, where they are confined to our central, eastern, and southern states. In the South, where they are found as far west as Texas, they operate on a 13-year cycle. The 17-year species are mainly northern.

These unique insects have extended the normal life span of two or three years to 13 and 17 years by staying underground in the juvenile stage for such periods. Then, all at virtually the same time (for each type), they dig their way out and change to the winged adult form. They live above ground for only a few weeks.

When the early settlers in America first encountered these insects, they were so impressed by their great numbers that they called them locusts—the only insect plague from the Old World that seemed comparable. Their appearance was first recorded in 1634 in the Massachusetts Bay Colony, and they are described in the first American

book on natural history, written by a Virginia clergyman
before the Revolution.

However, these American insects are not locusts (which
are grasshoppers). They are a quite different insect, about
four centimeters (approximately an inch and a half) long,
with two pairs of transparent wings and no such hopping
legs as has the grasshopper. As is often the case when confronted with a new and strange creature, people soon in-
vented myths to go with the cicada. If one looks carefully
at the wings of the adult, one sees that the veins near the
tips of the front wings make a little W. For the super-
stitious, W stands for "War," and thus the cicadas seemed
to be heralds of disaster. Since there is almost always a
war going on somewhere in the world, the myth seems to
be substantiated every 17 years for the believers in legends.

Toward the end of the last century, when the 17-year
cycle was first discovered, naturalists began to study the
cicadas to find out what was myth and what was truth
about them. There were found to be three species and a
number of different broods, and each one has its own 17-
or 13-year cycle. Some broods are larger and some smaller
and they sometimes overlap in their territories. But all
follow an exact 17- or 13-year period. Scientists interested
in the cicadas are still identifying new broods and territories. Thus, every year there are cicadas emerging somewhere across their wide range. Brood No. 1 was identified
in 1902, and there are now 19 broods located and charted
on maps of the eastern United States. Unbroken histories
of some broods have been compiled by checking records
as far back as 1715.

When the time approaches for a brood to make its appearance above ground, the white nymphs (as the juveniles are called) abandon the little oval chambers where they have lived so long among the roots of the trees and dig their way upward. There they pause, just below the surface, until some inner urge drives them to finish emerging. Sometimes they build little turrets above their holes, which may make their emergence easier. Sometimes they hide under stones. For they are helpless and vulnerable creatures. In the adult form they can fly, but do so sluggishly. Their only defense, the thing that insures the survival of the species, is their great numbers. When they emerge, at almost the same time, there are so many millions that the predators cannot possibly eat them all.

The Red-Eyed Ghost

The white, crawling nymphs are even more vulnerable, and so they wait till evening before coming out of their holes. They find the nearest tree and start climbing up. They climb until they find a secure hold, often well up in the tree or out on a branch. There they fasten themselves; the great transformation will soon take place. In about an hour, the skin splits down the back and the adult cicada wriggles out. The process takes anywhere from 20 minutes to three hours. At first the new cicada is white with red eyes. Its wings are small and crumpled. As it hangs on its perch or perhaps struggles higher in the tree, its wings expand and its color darkens. Finally it becomes a black insect with red eyes and orange legs and wing veins.

Soon after emergence, the males begin to make their familiar droning, whirring sound. The females are quiet, but the males make up for it with their mating calls. For the month or so that they are alive and above ground, they make their presence known with the loud buzzing that seems to come in waves. Like the sound of the sea, it never stops during the daytime. People ask, "How long is this going to go on?" It goes on until the cicadas have ended the business of mating and laid eggs for the new generation, after which the old generation disappears. No more is heard of them for another 13 or 17 years.

Mating takes place about a week after the cicadas emerge, and the female begins to lay eggs about a week after that. She has a sharp ovipositor, or egg-laying organ, at the end of her abdomen with which she pierces the bark of the tree so that she can lay her eggs inside. Two to ten small eggs are laid in a row. Then she pulls out the ovipositor and lays another row nearby. It takes her about 45 minutes to make such a "nest." When she has done this four or five times, she stops to rest. She has between 400 and 600 eggs to lay, and by the time she has completed this work, she is exhausted. She dies soon after.

What Happens to Trees

People are more keenly aware of the male cicada, because of the noise he makes. But it is the female that does the damage. When she makes her slit in the twig or branch and lays her eggs, the sap no longer reaches the outer leaves of that twig. They dry up and hang down. Sometimes the twig breaks completely and the leaves fall to the ground. This damage is clearly visible throughout the woods in a cicada year. Brown patches appear everywhere in the trees. In a forest, this is not serious. The damage is repaired the following year with new growth. Some scientists consider it nature's way of pruning the trees. However, in a domestic orchard the damage can often be serious. Nurserymen, orchardists, and home gardeners fear the work of the cicadas. In such cases, some control may be necessary. But considered overall, the periodical cicada is an inoffensive insect that bothers us only once in 13 or 17 years. There are also various broods of other cicada species with shorter life spans—so that some cicadas are present every summer—but bad damage is not likely to result from these.

Cicada eggs are laid in June and they hatch from mid-July through August. As each egg hatches and the infant insect crawls out, the one behind it must push out the empty shell before it too can escape. The nymphs are white, no bigger than ants, and just as lively. They fall to the ground and lose no time in entering the soil. They dig

During its underground stay the cicada nymph grows slowly through the years by feeding on tree rootlets, and occasionally enlarges its cell to accommodate its increasing size.

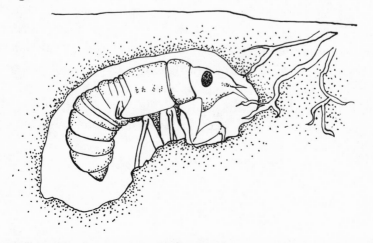

their way down for six to eighteen inches, until they find a good spot near the smallest roots of a tree. Each nymph makes itself a cell, smoothing it inside and strengthening it with a secretion which hardens the soil around it. It sinks its beak, much like a drinking straw, into the rootlet, and begins to feed. Here it stays, alternately resting and eating, while it gradually grows larger. Five times during its 17 years below ground, the nymph must shed its skin. It also occasionally enlarges its cell. Scientists have found as many as 20,000 cast-off skins of these cicada nymphs clinging to the roots of one small tree.

By the time the nymphs have shed their last skins underground, 17 years will have passed (or 13 for those in the South) and soon they will be ready to emerge into the air and repeat the cycle of mating, egg-laying and dying. Scientists are still studying this amazing insect. Perhaps it may have something to teach us about how to extend our life span. But why 17 and 13 years? Dr. Stephen J. Gould of Harvard University thinks that perhaps it has something to do with survival and escape from predators. Thirteen and 17 are prime numbers that cannot be divided evenly. As he sees it, they do not represent a series that some predator could learn and copy, thus building a habit of being on hand just when the nymphs emerge. Furthermore, they cover a long enough period of time so that most individual predators (birds, insects, small mammals) would be dead before the next brood emerged, and a possible memory, in mammals at least, would not be a factor. Whatever the answers may be, there are still plenty of questions about this extraordinary insect to keep biologists busy.

3

How Long Do Amphibians and Reptiles Live?

Amphibians are those adaptable creatures that live both in water and on land. Looking at them, we see a faint picture of how it must have been millions of years ago, when the first sea-dwellers climbed out upon the land and began to take over the new environment. There are two main classes of amphibians: the salamanders (Urodela) and the frogs and toads (Salientia). While the adult amphibians have learned to live on land (and some of them do so to a greater degree than others), they usually go back to water to lay their eggs. All the eggs are laid in an envelope or ribbon of jelly, which protects them until they hatch. And most larvae and all tadpoles stay in the water while they grow and transform into the adult animal.

While the eggs of all amphibians look very much alike, the larvae and tadpoles are very different. Often the young amphibians look nothing like the adults they will become, and like the insects must go through metamorphosis as they grow to adulthood. Salamander larvae have the long shape of their parents. At birth they have external gills and so can breathe in the water. The species that are born on land have minute gills which soon disappear. As the larva grows, its front legs appear and then the hind legs. The gills shrink and the tail becomes longer.

Children-Adults

A peculiarity of the salamanders is that some species never fully change into the adult form. This is a condition called neoteny—the holding over of the infantile characteristics into adult life. Two of our neotenous salamanders have been recorded as remarkably long-lived. Amphiuma is listed at 26 years, and Siren at 25 years. Amphiuma looks so much like an eel that the popular name for it is the Congo eel. But it is not a fish, as the word "eel" would imply. If one looks closely, it is clear that it has four very small feet, one pair just behind the head and the other near the tail, at the end of its long, snakelike body.

The greater siren (*Siren lacertina*) is another salamander that has the appearance of an eel. It has only one pair of legs, situated right behind the head. It also retains its external gills. This salamander grows to be three feet long, and while its shape seems to be all tail, in reality it has a long body with only a small tail at the end. It almost seems as though this ability to keep the youthful form must have some bearing on the life span, for the amphibian with the longest recorded life is a neotenous salamander from Japan. The giant salamander (*Megalobatrachus maximus*), found in western China and Japan, is credited with 52 years. It is a relative of the American hellbender (*Cryptobranchus alleghaniensis*), which has been known to live for 29 years. The giant salamander grows to be four feet long and may weigh 60 pounds.

Even though these neotenous salamanders never attain the adult form, they carry on all the activities of adults, mating, laying eggs, and reproducing their kind.

It is known that metamorphosis in the amphibians is regulated by the thyroid gland. But this does not clear up the mystery of why the neotenous salamanders never complete the change into adult forms. Scientists have proved that these animals have well-functioning thyroids. Thyroid extract has been injected into tadpoles and the larvae of nonneotenous salamanders. In all such cases, the larvae at once begin the process of transformation. But no amount of thyroid will make a neotenous salamander complete the change into an adult. Apparently certain tissues are immune to the effects of thyroid, so that the animal always retains its gills, infant teeth, skin, and other juvenile characteristics.

There are no neotenous frogs or toads, perhaps because the larval form is so different from the adult. Unlike the situation of the salamander larva, which keeps its external gills until it becomes adult, the gills of the tadpole soon move inside the body and then disappear when the creature develops lungs. Tadpoles mostly eat plants, whereas salamander larvae always eat meat. These larvae also have true teeth, but tadpoles have a horny beak with which they hold onto aquatic vegetation or break off pieces to eat.

The Life of Toads and Frogs

Even without neoteny, the frogs and toads can live to a fair life span when compared to many mammals. Of course, it is the unusual animal that completes this span.

Mortality is very high among the amphibians. Their eggs and young provide food for many other creatures. And even the adults are constantly in danger. They have few defenses except concealment and a quick getaway. Salamander young are usually solitary, hiding under stones and leaves. But the larvae of toads and frogs live in large groups. Often a spring rain will coincide with their emergence from the water. Suddenly there are little frogs everywhere, so that people say, "It's raining frogs!" Coming out onto a wet land is perhaps easier for these creatures that have always lived in the water. Immediately they face a great many dangers. Predators are everywhere. Dozens of young toads may set off across country to find a suitable home, and the first thing they do is cross a road. Most of them die under the wheels of cars. Nevertheless,

The smaller frogs may live from 12 to 20 years, but in the wild they seldom are lucky enough to escape predators that long.

the few individuals that survive these hazards live to grow up and learn to be wary.

The following year they return to the water where they must lay their eggs. Different species are more water-living than others. And some take longer to mature than the usual single season. A toad does not return to the water for mating and egg-laying until it is three or four years old. On the other hand, the bullfrog stays in the tad-pole stage for two seasons and sometimes even three. But the bullfrog can live from eight to ten years in the wild and up to 16 in captivity. And one toad has set a record of 36 years. Compare this with some mammals: rats and mice, up to five years; dogs that are old at ten.

Most people consider toads ugly, because of their lumps and bumps and dull brown color. But this appearance is really a wonderful camouflage; it is perhaps the trait most likely to insure it a long life. A toad spends most of its adult life in fields and gardens, and what could look more like a clod of earth than its warty skin?

The American toad is quite harmless. Though its skin has poison glands, simply handling it does no harm; the poison would have to get into the eyes, mouth, or blood to do damage. There are few animals as engaging as young toads. The animal is a useful adjunct to a garden. It helps to keep down many destructive insects and other crea-tures. Watching a toad eat is an experience in itself. It sits on its haunches until it sees something move. Suddenly, without warning, it's long tongue shoots out and in, and the fly or slug that was making its way along a leaf has dis-appeared. The toad's sticky tongue is fastened to the front of its mouth and lies curled up toward the back. It can shoot out to a remarkable distance, and the toad has a good aim.

As far as is known, salamanders do not have ears and do not hear in the sense that we do. But all the toads and frogs have ears and also voices. Anyone living in the country is aware of the many voices of these creatures. The first sounds to herald spring are the chirps of the spring peepers, one of our many species of tree frogs (Hylidae). Later in the spring we hear the deep boom of the bullfrog. The male toad also has a special song. He sings when he goes to the water to find a mate and fertilize her eggs. His call has been described as the sweetest of all: a high trill and at the same time a low droning note. He sings both day and night, but if the weather gets cold he may stop until it is warm again.

The male toad is so anxious to find a mate that sometimes he clings to rocks or another male toad. However, he soon discovers his error. The female toad is larger than the male and at mating time she is swollen with her great quantity of eggs—between 4000 and 20,000. She comes up to a singing male and pushes against him. At once he grabs her and climbs onto her back. She then moves out into the water and finds a spot that suits her. The couple submerge; she lays her eggs in a long string of jelly and he ejects the sperm to fertilize them. But they emerge every now and then for air. The male frog or toad has such a strong grip on his female that it is almost impossible to separate them. This is probably a good thing, because in some cases it takes from three to 26 days before all the eggs are laid, and the two must stay together all that time.

A *giant Galápagos tortoise* Testudo elephantopus, *now in the San Diego Zoo in California. These animals can live to over 100 years. Note the eye shape and stark white eyeballs, which suggest human eyes.*

The Reptiles and Their Ages

Perhaps the longest-lived creatures in the world live on a group of volcanic islands known as the Galápagos, which means "tortoise islands" in Spanish. Until these islands were discovered by the Spaniards in the sixteenth century, the giant tortoises (*Testudo elephantopus*) had no natural enemies and so were able to grow to a great size and to live to a remarkable age. Dr. Comfort lists *elephan-*

*topu*s at 100 plus years, but much longer has been claimed. On the other side of the globe, in the Indian Ocean, are several islands: Aldabra, Mauritius, and the Seychelles group—where giant tortoises of a related species are to be found. One of these, *Testudo sumeiri* is known to have lived to 152 years.

The Galápagos Islands, which lie approximately on the equator and some 600 miles from the South American mainland, are famous as the place where Charles Darwin first shaped his theory of evolution, which was a clear-cut focusing of various earlier and vaguer evolutionary theories. He stopped there in 1835 while voyaging on the exploratory ship *Beagle,* and was immediately impressed by the variety of animal and bird life peculiar to the islands and found nowhere else in the world. How had they come there? How had they adapted to their harsh environment?

Scientists are still arguing about how the giant turtles got there. Their nearest relatives are in South America, 600 miles away. Birds and insects could fly or be carried by the wind. Sea animals swam or were brought by the ocean currents. But these tortoises are land-dwellers. Fossils of giant tortoises have been found in both North and South America. Those in the north belong to an earlier era (the Eocene, 40 to 60 million years ago). The South American fossils are a mere 10 to 25 million years old (the Miocene), leading scientists to believe that the animals migrated from north to south. During much of that time there was no Central American land bridge, which suggests that perhaps those ancient animals somehow crossed the ocean.

So it seems that the present tortoise population on the Galápagos must have come by sea. Whether they came as small young turtles, marooned on floating vegetation, or as large tortoises that had somehow fallen into the sea, the ocean currents could have brought them to their new home in about two weeks.

Burning Sun and Cool Springs

The Galápagos Islands are not a place for easy living. The tropical sun has burned the coastal areas into a rocky desert where little besides cactus can grow. Only the larger islands have springs, and these are inland at higher elevations. The tortoises are always going to or from the springs to drink, and have made well-beaten paths leading outward from the water holes. Tortoises require a lot of water and when they first arrive at a spring, they rush to bury their heads in the water and gulp it down. They are especially fond of the prickly pear cactus and also eat desert grass and other vegetation that grows on the islands. They are supposedly vegetarians, but more recent observers have reported their eating the remains of a goat, and a captive tortoise was said to have caught and eaten two live rats.

There are two distinct types of tortoises in the Galápagos, and also there are definite variations in the populations on the different islands, so that a person well acquainted with the animals can tell which island an individual tortoise came from. Tortoises originally inhabited 11 islands in the archipelago, but they are now extinct on four of them, leaving only seven with tortoise populations.

The two main types of tortoises are those with a dome-shaped carapace (upper shell) and those with a narrow shell, flared out and upward and said to resemble a Spanish saddle. The dome-shaped individuals inhabit areas where the vegetation is more abundant and they can eat grass and low vegetation easily within their reach. The saddle-back type, which has developed longer legs and necks, lives in the desert regions, where the animals must feed on sparse growths and reach up to drooping branches of the giant prickly pear cactus. At evening they move into the grass or other growth and by pushing from side to side make themselves a bed for the night.

Courtship and Mating

Males are usually larger than females, and at mating time—February through April—there are many battles. Heaving themselves up on their pillar-like legs, each tries to reach higher than his opponent and to strike down on the other's head. Like knights in armor, they charge each other from a distance of six feet, pulling in their heads just before they collide.

When a male finds a female, he is said to circle her and smell her tail. Approaching her at right angles, he raises himself as high as he can and lets himself fall down on her with a thud. When he mounts her from the rear, he is often so much larger that his feet can reach the ground on both sides. During copulation, the male is reported to grunt and roar, making a noise that can be heard a great distance away. Eager males have even been seen trying to mate with large rocks.

In April or May, when the wet season is coming to an end, the females gather in certain nesting areas. They arrive with their bladders full of water, and after selecting a site, each individual will urinate, creating a muddy patch. Then she places a hind foot in the mud and by pressing and turning around, she makes a hole some seven inches across and eight to ten inches deep. Here she lays from seven to 20 white, round eggs, as big as billiard balls. When she has finished laying, she sits upon the nest and by moving back and forth causes her undershell to smooth out the mud over the eggs, making a flat cover, level with the surrounding soil. This cover dries in the sun and becomes as hard as clay. Sometimes the female scatters a layer of dirt between each layer of eggs. Often she goes on to make several more nests and lay eggs in each. Some observers give the incubation period as 161 to 246 days, but others insist that it takes as long as 13 months before the young turtles appear.

All the pushing and scraping at the nest may well break some eggs, and the hard clay, baked by the sun, often makes it difficult for the small turtles to find their way out. Some scientists think that a good rain is needed to help them emerge and that otherwise they may remain sealed in the nest till they die. Such arid nests have been dug up, to reveal dead and even mummified hatchlings. So it seems that many eggs and nestlings die before they can emerge into the light of day. However, since these long-lived creatures probably have a reproductive life of over 50 years, there would be no reason for their population to decrease.

An adult Galápagos tortoise with four hatchlings nearby. Parents of these tortoises do not care for or instruct their young.

Size and Age

Turtles grow very fast when young and become mature at an early age. After that, growth slows to a minimum, so that size is no criterion for judging the age of an individual. Archie Carr, the eminent herpetologist, cites a specimen of *Testudo vicina*, brought from the Galápagos when it weighed only 29 pounds, and which grew to weigh 450 pounds in only 15 years. Similar turtles, weighing only 26.5 pounds when captured, had grown to an average weight of 63 pounds each within a year.

There is much argument about the ages of turtles. Everyone agrees that they can live to a great age, but how great that age may be cannot be proved unless the individual turtle is kept under observation from birth. When they get older, their shells become worn and early growth rings are scraped off. Older tortoises living near the summit of one of the Galápagos volcanoes were noted to have deep scars on their carapaces, as though from falling lava or ash of an eruption. And since any eruption there must have happened a very long time ago, it is suggested that this shows the turtles' great age. But this is still not exact proof.

These remarkable animals lived undisturbed in their island paradise until the discovery of America. During the nearly 500 years since that event, they have been brought to the verge of extinction. The greatest of all predators, human hunters, had arrived. Now their numbers have been drastically reduced on the islands they still inhabit.

At first it was the Spaniards and the pirates in the sixteenth and seventeenth centuries who did the harm. Any ship stopping at the islands for water also took aboard a good-sized cargo of tortoises. These were usually stowed on their backs in a corner of the deck and were slaughtered as they were needed for food. Sometimes they were boiled down to make oil. In later centuries the islands were visited by whaling ships, which also took their toll. Over 5000 were taken by American whalers between 1811 and 1844, according to ships' records.

Intruders

By the twentieth century most of these depredations had ceased, but another threat to the turtles had developed. Beginning in the years of discovery, seamen made a practice of populating desert islands with such animals as pigs and goats. It was thought they would provide food for future shipwrecked sailors. By the twentieth century, a variety of these domestic animals had been imported to the Galápagos. Now there were wild donkeys and cats, as well as pigs and goats. On some islands there were even wild dogs, cattle, and horses; and that inveterate but unwished-for companion of travelers, the rat. The goats and donkeys competed with the tortoises for the scarce vegetation. The cats and rats and pigs dug up their eggs and ate the young hatchlings. If possible, these animal invaders were more often lethal than the earlier hunters, for now the turtles were unable to increase their numbers.

Even the scientists added to the toll. Fearing that the remarkable tortoises would soon become extinct, the New York Zoological Society in 1928 took away 180 turtles for breeding stock, sending them to zoos throughout the world. But efforts to breed the giants in captivity have not been very successful. Most zoos prefer to exhibit males, as they are bigger and more spectacular. The San Diego Zoo, which has the largest collection, found that only 10 per cent of the eggs were fertile and that only 7 per cent hatched. By 1960 only 122 of these tortoises were still alive in zoos.

However, the situation is not as bad as had been feared in 1928. The government of Ecuador, which owns the Galápagos Islands, spurred on by scientific and nature-loving people, has passed laws to protect the tortoises. Today the islands are a national park and nature reserve, and steps are being taken to clear out the alien animals and to protect the turtles. There is also the Darwin Research Station, built on the islands in recent years and financed by international conservation funds. Here scientists come to study the unique plant and animal life of the islands, and special attention is being given to the giant tortoises. Not only are they being studied for their physiology and behavior, but steps are being taken to protect the eggs and increase their numbers. On islands where it is impossible to eradicate the rats and other predators, the turtle eggs are collected and incubated and the young turtles raised in a safe place until they are large enough to be returned to their island.

This is a welcome change, and fortunately it has come in time for the wildlife of the Galápagos. On the islands of the Indian Ocean, where once related species of giant tortoises lived, things have not gone so well. Unlike the volcanic islands of the Galápagos, the Seychelles, Mauritius, and Aldabra support a lush vegetation and have thriving human populations, spreading out more and more to take over the wild habitat. Today, wild tortoises are found only on Aldabra. The few that live in captivity on the other islands were brought there from abroad and it is now hard to prove which island they originally came from.

Aged Box Turtles

We need not go as far away as the Galápagos Islands to find a long-lived turtle. Our own box tortoise (*Terrapene carolina*) can live to a ripe old age if given the chance. Of course, they are pygmies compared to the giants of the Galápagos. An adult male, maturing at four to five years, can measure about 14 by 11½ centimeters (approximately 5½ by 4½ inches), with a shell that is some 7½ centimeters (about 2⅞ inches) high. It has colorful markings on a black or brown shell; while the male has red eyes, the female's are light brown. The females are usually larger than the males.

Box turtles can be seen scrabbling through the woods or making their way across meadows, or even in the dangerous activity of crossing a road. They are found all over New England and the eastern United States, as far south as the Carolinas and Georgia and west to the Mississippi. However, the individual tortoise does not wander far from the area where it was hatched. One was found only a quarter of a mile from the spot where the finder's father had marked it 60 years earlier. Individuals have been caught with dates carved into their shells, suggesting an even greater age. But this cannot be taken as positive proof, since we cannot be sure that the date was accurate when first marked on the shell. Still, there is no doubt that these creatures live to a very old age. Archie Carr gives their life expectancy as 40 to 50 years, and Alex Comfort lists three that attained the ages of 118, 123, and even 129 years.

Eggs are laid in June and July, often in cultivated fields, where the soil is easily dug up. The female may take six to 14 hours to dig her nest, scooping out the soil with her hind feet. When she has dug a hole about three inches deep and two inches wide, she begins to lay her eggs. The clutch varies from three to eight eggs, and each egg is covered separately by the hind foot. When she is finished, she fills in the hole and smooths it over with her bottom shell (the plastron). It takes the eggs about three months to hatch.

Mating begins as soon as the tortoises come out of hibernation, usually in April. The males fight with each other and push the females around. They rise as high as they can on their legs and bite and snap at their opponents.

Water and Mud

The box tortoise is considered a land animal, but it will not hesitate to enter the water, and the younger ones are especially fond of getting into a pond or stream. If frightened, they will go to the water as a means of escape and can swim pretty well. The shell buoys them up and allows them to float, and while their swimming efforts may seem awkward, in time they get where they are going. In addition to crossing streams, box turtles have been seen swimming in the ocean.

In very hot weather, these tortoises like to bury themselves in mud, and some scientists believe that they estivate (go into summer sleep). They have been found buried six to ten inches deep in mud, where they apparently stay for weeks, as the mud around the entrance holes remains undisturbed, even drying out when the rains cease. There are reports of large gatherings of these turtles coming together in a muddy hollow to pass the hot weather in their individual burrows.

It is generally believed that the box turtle is deaf. Observers have noticed that no amount of shouting from the rear disturbs them. But if they see motion they promptly withdraw into their shells.

The box turtle eats a variety of food, both vegetable and animal. They relish insects, snails, and worms. They also eat moss, roots, mushrooms, grass, leaves, seeds, and berries. They have been known to kill toads and small snakes. They drink a lot of water, usually keeping the head submerged while drinking.

The adult box turtles have little to fear, as their heads, tails and legs can be completely drawn into the shells and the edges closed so tightly that no predator can get in. But eggs and infant turtles are often eaten by skunks. Young box tortoises have been found in the stomachs of crows.

The box turtle is considered edible, but we seldom use it as food. In one instance, during a miner's strike in Pennsylvania, food was so scarce that the men caught turtles in the woods and ate them. They all became sick, and it was thought that the turtles might have been eating toadstools, which made their flesh poisonous. If left alone, the animal is beneficial to humans; it eats a great quantity of injurious insects and grubs. About the only misdemeanor charged against it is occasional sampling of melons in the field.

4

The High and Varied Fliers

Among the birds, the potential for living long seems to be very roughly related to size. The larger birds undoubtedly live longer than the smaller. But when we consider the overall size of birds compared with the rest of the animal kingdom, this relationship must be discarded. The smallest bird, the hummingbird, has established records of eight years in two captive species. Compared to the approximate spans for the much larger rats and mice (four and three years), this is remarkable.

Birds have a much higher metabolism than mammals. Their hearts may beat faster than 400 times a minute, compared with only about 70 per minute in people. When the bird is in flight, the heart may beat more than 1000 times a minute. A bird's blood may circulate completely in less than a second, whereas it takes eight seconds in humans. They also have a high rate of food consumption. Many birds must eat 80 per cent of their body weight each day. Whether this difference in metabolism has any bearing on the difference in life spans is unknown.

Songbirds may live 10 to 15 years in captivity, though two to three years is their average. There is a record of a chaffinch that lived to be 29 years old. Pigeons often live for 30 to 40 years. For large predators, such as eagles, owls, and vultures, life is still longer. While the proven age is not always spectacular, there are many cases of reported ages that are really extraordinary. Cranes, geese, and ostriches are also credited with long life. But the birds that have perhaps the greatest reputation for reaching ripe old age are the parrots, and in their case the facts live up to their reputation. The cockatoos of Australia, the macaws of the Americas, and the parrots of Africa all enjoy an extended life span.

The bird at the top of Dr. Comfort's list is the eagle owl of Europe, with a proven age of 68 years. There is also a record of 55 years for the African snake eagle (*Terathopsius ecaudatus*) and one of 42 years for the Chilean eagle (*Geranoaëtus melanoleucus*). The fish owl of Ceylon (*Ketupa zeylonensia*) has a record of 39 years. Next comes the greater sulphur-crested cockatoo, with 56 years. And there was the case of a mute swan which was shot in England in 1887 and found to be wearing a leg ring indicating it was 170 years old. But since scientifically organized bird-banding did not get under way until this century, this record must be viewed with some distrust, like the dates carved on turtles' shells.

Hummingbirds: Living at High Speed

There are over 300 species of hummingbirds and they are found only in the New World. While a number of them come into the western United States, only the ruby-throated hummingbird (*Archilochus colubris*) visits the

AUSTRALIAN INFORMATION SERVICE

Parrots are long-lived. These are green leek parrots, Polytelis swainsonii; *they are brilliant green with a scarlet breast.*

eastern part of the country. It is so small that it is often taken for an insect. In fact, there is a group of moths called hummingbird moths because they so closely resemble the bird.

The male ruby-throat is spectacular, but he flies so fast that one must look quickly to keep him in view. Usually he appears hovering over a flower in search of nectar. His back is iridescent green and the throat beneath his long, pointed beak has a bright red patch. His wings move so fast that one sees only a blur, and they make a buzzing sound, which gives the bird its name.

The hummingbird is the only bird that can fly backward. It can fly off at any angle and can stand perfectly still in the air, hovering over the spot that has claimed its attention. This bird lives at such a high rate of metabolism (all the chemical processes in an organism that provide energy and control) that it needs constant nourishment to replace the energy it is using up. If food is not available, it will quickly die. It is perhaps comparable to the shrew, one of the smallest mammals. Every 24 hours, the shrew must eat its weight in food. But it has nothing like the possible eight-year life expectancy of the hummingbird. In most cases it dies after 15 or 16 months.

Perhaps one way that the hummingbird has met this problem of metabolism is its ability to slow down its vital functions at night. It achieves a kind of hibernation, called torpidity. In this condition, the birds can be picked up and moved from perch to perch or laid out on a table as though dead. By reducing its breathing and heartbeat, the bird saves energy that would otherwise have to be made up with additional food. However, scientists have noticed that when incubating her eggs, the female hummingbird does not become torpid but sleeps normally, so her body warmth protects the eggs at that time.

The sexes have little to do with each other except at mating time, when the male displays his glowing plumage to the female and puts on a show of aerial acrobatics. He dive-bombs her from eight to ten feet up, missing her by a few inches and swooping up to repeat the act from the other side. When the female has accepted him, they perform a sort of dance together, facing each other and flying up and down almost vertically to a height of five or six feet. One observer says that when the male was at the top of his flight, the female was at the bottom, and vice versa. Their tails were spread and they were twittering at each other as they stayed about two and a half feet apart.

Usually the work of nest-building and rearing the young is done by the female alone. The nests are so small that they are hard to find, looking like nothing more than a knot on the branch of a tree. Often it is built over water. The nests are made of bud scales, lichens, plant down, and spider silk. The silk is used to bind it all together and to fasten it to the tree limb, which often is no more than an inch in diameter. The plant down, such as the down of thistles, is caught by the bird while it is flying about in the air, and used to line the nest.

Two eggs are laid, and when the young first hatch they are no bigger than a pea and quite naked. They are fed by regurgitation. As their beaks are quite short when the infants are hatched, the mother bird, perched on the rim of the nest, pokes her long needle-like bill straight down into the infants' throats. Nectar is not the only food that young hummingbirds get. Small spiders and insects that live in the flowers are also part of the diet. When the hatchlings grow bigger and their beaks become longer, the mother pokes the food in from the side.

Hummingbirds have few natural enemies, and they are so quick and alert that they can avoid most predators. In addition, they are so small that they are hardly worth the effort a predator must exert to catch them. Occasionally one of the smaller hawks may take one, and a few extraordinary accidents have been reported. One hummer became caught in a spider's web (and was rescued by an investigator when the spider was already binding it up with webbing). Another ruby-throat was found stuck on the points of a thistle. But undoubtedly the greatest hazard these little creatures face is the weather. If the birds fly north too quickly they may outrun the spring and find themselves in a region where the flowers have not yet opened. And even in the most glorious springtime, a sudden frost can arrive, killing all the flowers. Cold and snow are destructive to the hummers, but often they can counter this with torpidity. It is the loss of their food supply that is most sure to kill.

The Remarkable and Charming Penguins

A bird that survives in a most hostile environment, battling the severest weather our atmosphere can produce, is the penguin. There are 17 species, and they live all over the southern hemisphere, coming as far north as the equator. But the largest populations breed on the Antarctic continent. Penguins are sea birds that have lost their

AUSTRALIAN INFORMATION SERVICE

Emperor penguins meet something new in their Antarctic life, a helicopter. These tough birds cope with weather conditions that humans consider almost impossible.

power of flight in favor of skillful swimming abilities, and they live most of their lives in the sea. But when the time comes to lay eggs and raise young, like all sea birds they must find a nesting place ashore. The emperor penguins and the Adélie penguins nest on the Antarctic continent. Other species go to such land areas in the southern hemisphere as New Zealand, Australia, South Africa, the Falkland Islands and the Galápagos.

The Adélie penguins (*Pygoscelis adeliae*) spend the winter months chasing their food, little shrimps known as krill, and they go to their breeding grounds in the spring. The largest of the penguins, the emperors (*Aptenodytes forsteri*), reverse the process and go ashore to raise their young in the dark, bitter Antarctic winter.

Only one egg is laid by the emperor, which the male bird incubates by holding it in a pouch under his feathers and on top of his feet. He carries it about with him in this manner for two months, the time required for the egg to hatch. During this whole period he does not eat, since the breeding ground is miles from open ocean. He incubates the egg alone, for as soon as she has laid it, the female leaves for the sea, walking miles to reach open water. She returns about the time the egg hatches. She comes full of fish, which she has been catching assiduously, and which she now regurgitates to feed the baby. The father penguin leaves immediately on his trek to the sea, where he also fills up on fish, bringing much of it back to feed his mate and the baby. This remarkable behavior is carried out in continuous night and under the most brutal weather our planet can inflict.

It is estimated that there are 300,000 emperor penguins nesting in 23 colonies, and it is believed that their mortality is greater while at sea than during their winter nesting period. There are few predators during the winter months in the Antarctic. The leopard seal is their greatest enemy and sometimes giant petrels, which stay in the Antarctic all winter, may take chicks. At sea, in addition to the leopard seal, they must face attacks by the killer whale and other marine predators.

The eminent paleontologist George Gaylord Simpson says that a record of 34 years has been set by an emperor penguin in a zoo. Considering the difficulties that zoos have had in keeping penguins alive in captivity, this seems like a fair indication of their potential life span.

Since the Adélie penguins do their nesting in the summer months, they have the benefit of sunlight. But even in summer, the Antarctic can produce violent storms, and when the birds first arrive in the spring they must walk over great stretches of frozen sea, sometimes as much as 60 miles, to reach their nesting sites. They also have an additional hazard in the skua, a predatory gull that breeds in the Antarctic at the same time as the Adélies and is quick to eat any eggs or chicks that are left unattended. In fact, some scientists think that the emperor may have taken up the habit of winter breeding to escape the attacks of the skua.

Adélie penguins lay two eggs and they build a nest of stones. There is often much quarreling and stealing of stones between one nesting couple and another. In the Antarctic there are no plants that can be used for nesting materials, but the stones serve to keep the eggs out of water, which sometimes collects if snow falls and then melts.

Most penguins go through all sorts of comical gestures and "dances" in order to find a new mate or to locate an old one. Penguins are usually monogamous, and while the couple may be far apart in their lives at sea, they return to the old nesting site each year and, if possible, to the same mate. When the male arrives at his old nesting area, he at once asserts his territorial claim. He stretches his neck as high as he can with the beak pointing toward the sky. He flaps his flippers and lets out a harsh caw. After a few such demonstrations, a female will run up to him. Often it is his old mate. If not, and the old mate arrives later, she evicts the newcomer. Sometimes the couple will display together. They stand face to face, wave their flippers and their necks and call raucously.

Like the emperors, the Adélie female goes to sea as soon as eggs are laid, leaving the father to incubate the eggs while she gathers food. But she is gone for a much shorter time, and returns in about two weeks. Spring is now advancing, the ice is melting and the open sea is coming closer to the rookery. The incubation period is shorter for the Adélies: about 35 days, but during that time the male and female change places several times. The chicks are fed about every other day with regurgitated food and may get as much as a pound and a half at a feeding.

When they are about four weeks old, the chicks leave the nests and congregate in large groups. Perhaps 100 chicks will bunch together. This is a protective device against the skuas. The chick that wanders off by itself is usually doomed. Parents go to sea for food and return to feed their chicks. It has been proved by marking the birds that each parent feeds its own chicks. But how they locate and recognize each other is something of a mystery. Probably each knows the other's voice, for if a returning adult does not at once find its own chick, it calls loudly and the chick comes running.

By the time the young have lost their infantile down and acquired their juvenile plumage, they are ready to take care of themselves, and the adult birds leave them, returning to the sea for the winter months. The young have to learn to swim on their own, and their first efforts to leap quickly out of the water to an ice cliff or rock are said to be comical.

L. E. Richdale, a New Zealand scientist, studied the yellow-eyed penguins that nest along the coasts of that island. He learned that this species, which begins to breed when it is two years old, can live for over 20 years.

The Parrots

There are over 300 species of parrot-like birds living around the world in tropical countries. Some are as short as nine centimeters (about three and a half inches) and some as long as a meter or so (about three and a half feet), measured from tip of bill to tip of tail. They all have large, hooked, down-curving beaks especially adapted for fruit-eating. But many use their beaks also to crack seeds, break open nuts, or dig roots. They are gaily colored birds, often green with bright patches of red and blue and yellow. They have four toes, two pointing forward and two backward. These are very useful for climbing about in trees. A parrot can get such a good grip on a branch with one set of claws that he can use the other set for picking up food and conveying it to his mouth. Their cries are loud and raucous, but they have a remarkable ability to mimic any sound they hear, whether it be a creaking door or human speech. They are very popular everywhere as pets.

Dr. Comfort lists several species of the parrot family on his roster of long-lived birds, and at the top is the greater sulphur-crested cockatoo (*Kakatoë galerita*) of Australia. Although a record of only 56 years is proven for this bird, there are reported cases of 69, 80, and 120 years. Cockatoos are large birds with long tails and showy feather crests which they can raise and lower, seemingly to express their emotions. Galerita is one of the largest, and as

AUSTRALIAN INFORMATION SERVICE

The galah, or rosebreasted cockatoo, is found only in Australia. It is a popular pet because it has a friendly nature and easily imitates human sounds.

All animals evolve some sort of protection against predators that leads to a longer life. Sometimes, as in the box turtle, it is an armored type of body and sometimes it is intelligence and alertness—or any combination of these. The pink cockatoo (right), Kakatoë leadbeateri, which feeds in large flocks, posts sentries first to warn of approaching danger. Notice its handlike use of one leg.

AUSTRALIAN INFORMATION SERVICE

its common name indicates, it has a yellow crest; the rest of it is white. It is a bold, flashy bird, usually seen flying over the forest or perching in the treetops in groups of three or four, and advertising its presence with loud, harsh cries.

A smaller bird, the rose-breasted cockatoo (*Kakatoë roseicapilla*), also called the galah, is credited with a life

span of 30 to 47 years. It is very widespread and abundant in Australia and flocks in open areas, often with other species of cockatoos. It likes to perch on telegraph wires, and the younger, inexperienced birds are sometimes killed by cars along the highways. These birds can be destructive to trees, stripping the bark in their search for food.

A third species of cockatoo, the slender-billed (*Licmetis tenuirostris*), has a proven span of 34 and a reported length of 85 years. This bird is much like the galah, but has a very long upper beak which it uses for digging up roots. It is usually found near water, making its nests in hollow trees along a stream. As it is a ground feeder, its beautiful under-plumage is often smeared with mud.

The American tropics are also the home of spectacular members of the parrot family. Many of these are long-lived birds. The blue and yellow macaw (*Ara ararauna*) has a record of 43 years, and the red and blue macaw (*Ara macao*) of 38, with a reported life of 64 years.

Anne Dunbar Graham, in her book *A Bird in My Bed* gives a charming picture of the mating rituals of one of the smaller parrots from Central America, Petz's conure. They are green birds with blue and yellow shadings, and they feed largely on fruit. They especially like the fruit of a tree known as the parrot fruit tree, which has large green fruits that somewhat resemble a parrot; when the birds are sitting in the tree it is hard to tell birds from fruit. No doubt this is a protection against predators, adding advantages for the life span of the species that would not be present if they were, say, bright red.

In the wild, these parrots like to build their nests in the homes of the tree-living termite Nasutitermes. The insects construct large oval balls of hardened mud, usually in oak trees. Both the male and female conure take part in digging out a hole in this ball. They begin low on the side of the ball and dig a tunnel going upward at an angle. When they reach the center, they turn the tunnel downward and dig a round nesting cavity. Instead of rushing out to defend their nest, as you might expect, the termites merely seal off all their little tunnels leading to the birds' excavations. Birds and insects seem to live peacefully together. The termites do not bite the birds, as they would any other invader, and the birds do not eat the termites. In fact, the termites often take over the conures' nest after they have deserted it. And it is said that the conures will not nest in a termitarium that has been deserted by its occupants.

Africa also has its share of interesting parrots. One of the best known is the African gray parrot, which has a proven life record of 49 years and a reported record of 73 years. Although its plumage is not as beautiful as that of many of the parrots, it is said to be the best mimic, and therefore very popular as a pet.

The Predators

Predatory birds are also high on Dr. Comfort's list of methuselahs. At the top is the eagle owl (*Bubo bubo*) with a proven record of 68 years. Behind that comes the snake eagle of Africa with 55, and our golden eagle, with 46 and a report of 80.

The eagle owl is similar to our great horned owl. There are 12 species of this genus spread around the world, and they are among the largest of all owls. *Bubo bubo* is native to Europe and Asia, but it is becoming scarce due to the encroachments of civilization.

This owl nests on the ground among inaccessible rocks or on a rocky ledge. They have been found 15,000 feet up in the Himalayas. The male brings food to the nest while the female sits on the eggs and protects the young. Hares, mice, rats, ducks, and other birds are favored. Bengt Berg, who photographed an eagle owl's nest in the 1950s, reported that the victims were mostly rats. These were all delivered minus their heads, and the female arranged them in neat rows at the back of the ledge. She often took time to rearrange the rows and piles of bodies.

In the nest that Berg observed, there were three young, all born blind. When they cried for food, the mother tore up a rat and stuffed the pieces down their open beaks. The youngest one was always the weakest and had trouble getting its share of the food. In the end, Berg removed this nestling and raised it at home. It turned out to be a female, and Berg found that the female's hoot is an octave higher than the male's.

Cleaning Up Organic Debris

The scavenger birds are also long-lived creatures. These, though meat eaters, do not kill their prey but eat only dead animals. People generally feel aversion for such birds and animals, but in truth they do a good job of cleaning up carcasses that would otherwise rot and pollute the environment; and they are not dangerous birds, as are some true predators.

The vultures all have huge wings well adapted for soaring. They spend the day floating round and round at great heights and their keen eyes can see everything that happens far below. When they see something that looks like a dead animal, they come down to investigate. Often there are a number of vultures soaring over a wide region, each over its own territory, and when one goes down, the others hasten to join it.

In the Americas, the largest of these vultures are the condors. The South American condor (*Vultur gryphus*) has a life-span record of 52 years, and the North American species (*Gymnogyps californianus*) one of 37 years. The California condor is on the verge of extinction. A 1977 estimate by the Audubon Society places their numbers at no more than 40, and great efforts are being made to protect and save the species.

Most vultures have no feathers on the head and neck, an adaptation that is very practical. They have weak claws, adapted for perching rather than for grasping prey, as are predators' claws. They have small beaks which are unable to tear up a fresh carcass. This is why vultures often sit around a dead animal for a period of time. They are waiting for the flesh to decompose so that they can tear it out more easily. In this process they must stick their heads right into the body. This is dirty work, and the lack of feathers on the head and neck is a safeguard for the bird. If neck feathers became matted with blood and carrion, it could not preen them off, and disease would develop.

The California condor has a wingspread of three meters (about ten feet) and weighs up to 11 kilograms

HUGH M. HALLIDAY

The inborn habits popularly called "instinct" are a great help to birds, as well as other animals, in the matter of surviving to an older age. These ruffed grouse chicks are staying utterly still ("freezing") while danger threatens them.

(about 25 pounds). It is one of the largest known birds, but its habitat has been gradually constricted until it now lives in only a small area in Santa Barbara and Ventura counties. It is a great black bird, with white wing markings; its bare head and neck are reddish orange. It breeds only every other year, for the nesting cycle is a long one. Five weeks are required to incubate two or three eggs, and another two to three months pass before the young are out of the nest. Even then it takes months for them to learn to fly well and to find their food. They are dependent on their parents for a long time.

In the Old World there is a variety of vultures, most of

which are found in the tropics. As the world becomes more civilized and fewer carcasses are left lying around, the vulture population declines. Also, the custom of putting out poisoned meat for wolves and other animals has killed many of these scavengers.

Africa is the home of many species of vultures. The Egyptian vulture is credited with a proven 23-year span and a reported one of 101 years. The griffon vulture of the Mediterranean has a proven record of 38 years and one reported for 117. And the king vulture is recorded at 40 years.

Like the vultures of the New World, these birds usually have naked heads and necks because of their habit of reaching into the decomposing carcasses for their food. They nest on high ledges or in trees, building big nests of sticks. They lay one or two eggs which require a long incubation period, and the young are in the nest for a long time.

A few species of vultures have evolved different eating habits. The palm-nut vulture has developed a liking for the fruit of the oil-palm tree. It augments this diet by an occasional dead fish. Perhaps it is this cleaner style of dining that has allowed it to evolve feathers on its neck.

The Bird and the Tool

The Egyptian vulture has the distinction of being one of the few birds known to use a tool. It is very fond of eggs, and it can lift the smaller eggs in its beak and smash them onto the ground. But in dealing with an egg as large as the ostrich's, this method will not work, for the vulture cannot pick it up, and the bird's rather weak bill can make no impression on the shell. These vultures have solved the problem by hitting the egg with stones.

The naturalist Dr. Jane Goodall was the first to observe this unusual habit. She and Hugo van Lawick were photographing wildlife in the Serengeti, when they noticed vultures dropping down to a point in the distance. They found a group of vultures fighting over a nest of some 20 ostrich eggs. The ostrich parents had been frightened away by an encroaching grass fire. Most of the vultures were struggling to eat the already broken eggs, but the scientists saw one bird pick up a stone and throw it at an unbroken egg. This is an extraordinary action for a bird, and the observers were astonished. They watched as the bird, after several hits and misses, made a crack in the shell and then broke the egg open with its beak. At once, the victor was set upon by the other vultures and the tool-user enjoyed only a small taste of his egg.

The scientists studied this unusual behavior in detail, setting up various situations to test the vultures. They believe that this remarkable behavior is not instinctive but has to be learned, for they observed a young vulture that tried for an extended period to crack open an ostrich egg with its beak. When it gave up, another bird moved in with a stone and quickly did the job.

5

Speaking of
Mammals . . .

As we have seen, mammals, considered to be highest on the evolutionary scale, do not live nearly as long as the reptiles, most of which died out as the mammals evolved. Even the birds do relatively better than the mammals. The shortest-lived mammals are small ones, those classed as rodents (rats, mice, hamsters, guinea pigs, squirrels, beavers, and others) and insectivores (moles, shrews, hedgehogs).

The extremely small carnivores called shrews are said to be the most aggressive animals known, considering their size. Although classed as insectivores, they also attack and eat larger creatures, such as mice, moles, lizards. They are very beneficial to the gardener in that they eat great quantities of harmful insects. Shrews have been known to destroy gypsy moth caterpillars on the grand scale. They will also eat each other if they are confined in close quarters.

Shrews weigh between $\frac{1}{15}$ and $\frac{2}{5}$ of an ounce, according to the species. They live at such a high rate of metabolism that they must eat every two hours, and this voracious appetite drives them to attack animals many times

VICTOR B. SCHEFFER

Like the shrew, the shrew mole is a voracious eater. A man eating at its rate would consume some 200 pounds a day.

their size. They move so fast that they are not easily seen and few predators can catch them. Some of the species have a poisonous bite that paralyzes their victims. The bite of the short-tailed shrew is especially toxic. Yet in spite of these protections against predators, their life in the wild is ordinarily around a year; the maximum is two years.

Jack Denton Scott has described a fishing trip on which one of his companions was bitten by a shrew. Scott had been watching a number of shrews dashing about the woods, and one even sniffed at his foot but did not find the leather boot attractive. However, a friend standing a short distance away had cleaned his boots with animal fat, and the shrew was excited by the smell. It ran up the man's boot and onto his trousers, where it bit him on the leg. Close examination showed that he had been bitten four times. His leg swelled and the unfortunate fisherman was sick for two days.

Shrews build a nest of grass in a burrow, in a stump, or under a log. This nest is shaped like a ball and may hold from three to seven young, which are no larger than a housefly. They are born naked, blind, and deaf, but the fur grows within two weeks. Then their ears begin to function and their teeth appear. Sight comes last, at about a month. The mother shrew, who evicted her mate before the nest was finished, chases out her young as soon as they can see. From that moment they must fend for themselves. Each little shrew makes its own way and lives entirely by instinct. It is never taught to hunt, as are most mammals. It simply does what comes naturally, to fill its stomach with anything it can find and assuage its all-consuming hunger. As we saw earlier, it has to eat its own weight in food every day in order to stay alive.

In spite of their short life, shrews reproduce at such a fast rate that their population remains stable. A zoo director reports a pair that produced 66 young in less than a year. The gestation period is from 12 to 16 days and a female can have a second litter 24 days after the first one.

Another example of a short-lived mammal is the long-tailed field mouse (*Apodemus sylvaticus*) that inhabits Europe, Asia, and North Africa. This little mouse with the big eyes is usually nocturnal. It is considered a pest, helping itself to the gardener's strawberries, bulbs, peas, and beans, which it carries into its underground nest and feeds on during the day. It also eats hazelnuts and acorns.

The nest is at the end of a tunnel and large enough to house several adults, for these mice are social animals. There are usually five young and the gestation period is 26 days. The female can have six litters a year and can begin breeding when it is only a few months old. The life expectancy of this mouse is said by one investigator to be hardly more than a year. However, two letters in 1977 issues of the British magazine *New Scientist* record captured field mice that lived for over two years. None of these two-year-old mice had shown any inclination to relinquish life at the time the letters were written. Another British rodent, the dormouse, can live for six years. Possibly its life span has been extended by its habit of hibernating during the winter.

As we consider larger mammals, we find longer life spans. Dr. Comfort says that domestic horses can live up to and beyond 40, and there is a record of a white mule in southern Nevada that led a band of mustangs for 55

DR. KLAUS SCHWARZ, VETERANS ADMINISTRATION

Mice in the wild seem to average around two years in life span; albino mice such as this one may live somewhat longer when kept as a pet. Rodents vary considerably in their life spans; a guinea pig, for instance, can live beyond seven years.

years until it was shot in 1965. There are a number of other surprises. Bats live much longer than might be expected. In recent years much work has been done with banding bats, much as is done with birds. Horseshoe bats have been recaptured after seven years, and there are records of their living for 16 years. Dr. Comfort says this is to be expected, as bats have a slow rate of reproduction, usually producing but one infant at a time, and that over a longer period than the mice and shrews, which have large litters in quick succession.

On the other hand, whales, among the largest mammals living, are believed to live only between 30 and 50 years at the most. The blue whale, the biggest of all animals, is mature at five, and none was found older than 12 years, according to reports published in 1937 and 1950. It is hard to be sure about whales and dolphins, as they have only recently come under scientific study. Unfortunately, at the rate these creatures are being slaughtered by fishermen and whalers, there may not be many years left in which they can be studied.

The Mighty Elephants

The animal that comes closest to humans in length of life is the elephant: 50 to 70 years, with occasionally a still older record. In fact, their development, age at maturity, and such statistics correspond so closely to our own that in India, where they are domesticated, a young elephant is usually given a boy of the same age to grow up with and act as its trainer and master. Often these men live their whole lives with their own special elephant, going with it and working with it wherever it may be sent.

It is generally accepted that there are two species of elephants, the Indian (*Elephas maximus*) and the African (*Loxodonta africana*). There are many striking differences between the two species, so it is quite easy to tell them apart. The African species is larger than the Indian, standing as much as 3.3 meters (some 11 feet) at the shoulder and weighing six tons. This is the largest living land animal, and the specimen at the Smithsonian museum in Washington measures about four meters (some 13 feet) in height. Females are somewhat smaller, weighing about four tons. The female of the African species has tusks, whereas the Indian cow does not.

The African elephant has large ears, a grooved trunk, a flat forehead, and the head is held higher than the back, which is concave. In the Indian elephant, the ears are much smaller, the trunk is smoother than the African's, the head has a domed forehead and the back is convex, rising above the head. As in bats and primates, the elephant's teats are located between the front legs. Most elephants seen in circuses are Indian elephants and they are usually cows, females being considered more tractable than the bulls.

Perhaps the most remarkable thing about the elephant is its trunk. This organ has evolved out of the upper lip and nose, and with it the animal can do a great variety of things. It is very strong and also very sensitive. At the end is a muscle called the finger with which the elephant can grasp and pick up even small objects. The Indian elephant has one finger and the African has two. Elephants do not eat or drink through their trunks, as uninformed persons may think. They use the trunk to pick up food and put it into their mouths, or to suck up water and siphon it down their throats.

Elephants once lived over a wide area of the earth's surface, and their fossil record goes back 50 million years. They were first domesticated in the Indus valley sometime between 2500 and 1500 B.C. Presumably the animals were first used to pull heavy loads and for general transport. But later it was found that they were very useful in war. Elephants are among the most peaceable animals on earth, so it is ironic that, like the horse, their chief use, until recently, has been in battle.

Elephants are not very effective domestic animals, for several reasons. They eat so much that only the wealthy can afford to maintain them. The work of ploughing and transport can be done as well by other domestic beasts, like the horse, the mule, or the ox. Only in dense jungles, where these animals cannot function, does the elephant come into its own. And that is where it is used today (aside from zoos and circuses): in the teak forests of eastern Asia. Tame elephants in such lumber camps are turned out periodically in the forest to feed themselves. These animals are very intelligent. Jack Denton Scott tells of riding through the jungle on the back of an elephant when his hat blew off. Without any orders from its mahout, or trainer, the elephant stopped, picked up the hat, and returned it to Scott.

It used to be thought that elephants would not breed in captivity, but this is not so. If given sufficient room and inducement, they will do so. But it is not practical to breed work elephants. Females are preferred in work camps, and if one becomes pregnant, she cannot be used for an extended time, as the gestation period is from 18 to 24 months. After birth the young elephant suckles for a year and follows the mother for five years. They do not become adult and workable until they are 16 years old.

Following Elephants for Five Years

Very little was known about the habits of the African elephant until recently. In 1965 a young Oxford zoologist went to Africa to study the elephants of Lake Manyara. It was thought that they were eating up their food supply, stripping the bark from trees so that soon there would be nothing left but scrub and wasteland. Some scientists favored the plan of shooting some of the elephants in order to reduce their numbers, as was being done in other parks. Others believed that the tree destruction was a natural process that had always gone on; that when the trees were

KENYA TOURIST OFFICE
Elephants are among the most peaceful of mammals. This is the African species, Loxodonta africana. *Ordinarily they reach about 70 years in age.*

gone, grassland would develop and then another type of forest. Nobody really knew the ecological answers, and so Iain Douglas-Hamilton was given the job of studying the elephants and their habitat.

Douglas-Hamilton worked on this study for five years. During that time he married and his wife came to assist him. He found that elephants live in family groups of an old matriarch, her daughters, a few young males, and all their calves. Often there are several such groups, related families, feeding and moving about close by. The young scientist learned to tell all these animals apart and he compiled lists of the families, the behavior of individuals, and their relationship to each other.

As he followed them about in an old Land Rover, taking photographs and making notes, he found that there was a great variation in the behavior of individuals. Following elephants in the wild is not the safest occupation, and Douglas-Hamilton had a number of frightening experiences before he learned what to expect from individual elephants. Among domesticated elephants, the male is considered the more dangerous and females are preferred. But in the wild, matters seem to be reversed. A solitary bull would go on eating and pay little attention to the Land Rover. But a female, guarding her family and young, was a different matter. A charge almost always ensued.

When the scientist had learned to recognize the individual elephants, he found that there were differing degrees of charges. He named one group of four large cows the Torone sisters, and he learned to stay a safe distance from them. They were inclined to attack without warning, without even a charge, and on one occasion they almost carved up his car while he and a friend were in it. On the other hand, a huge matriarch, whom he named Boadicea, gave every sign of aggressive intent, flapping her ears, curling up her trunk, trumpeting and then charging in a most terrifying manner. But just before she made contact with the car, she would swerve aside and attack a nearby bush, in a fine display of what is called redirected aggression. Douglas-Hamilton used to exhibit this behavior to visitors at his camp, as an example of the hazards of elephant-watching. And movie-makers who wanted to photograph a charging elephant were always brought to Boadicea's group.

Elephantine Cows and Calves

Fundamentally, elephants are peaceful creatures, seldom fighting among themselves, and showing the greatest affection for members of their own group. They greet each other with their trunks, putting that appendage in the other animal's mouth, or patting each other with it. The mother uses her trunk to reassure her newborn calf or to keep contact with it as it stands beneath her belly to suck. Older cows often have several calves of various ages following them around, and these show great interest in a new infant, patting it with their trunks and standing over it protectively.

After the first two days, the youngest one is able to walk without constantly falling down and to keep up with the herd as it moves from one feeding ground to another. But it takes longer than that for it to learn to handle its trunk. Young elephants are said to be quite comical as they try to figure out what to do with this strange appendage, and Douglas-Hamilton observed one of them sitting down with its trunk in its mouth, sucking much as a child sucks its thumb.

Elephant herds are made up chiefly of cows and their calves. The males wander off by themselves and turn up only at breeding time. But family feeling among the cows is very strong, and if one dies, another female in the group will take on the care of her infants. Douglas-Hamilton has

*An African mother elephant helps its calf to cope with a
steep bank.*

told most movingly of a cow that had died and left three
offspring of varying ages. One day as he walked in the
forest, he heard the loud bawling of an elephant calf and
hastened to find out the reason. He then saw that the cow
had missed her footing on a hillside and fallen down a
steep slope. She was obviously dead, and was surrounded
by her three calves. The oldest was moaning in grief,
every once in a while giving vent to an emotional howl.

The second stood silently, leaning against the mother, and the smallest, of less than a year, was trying pathetically to nurse. The scientist watched this tragic scene for about 15 minutes, till the wind changed and the animals caught his scent. Then they turned and forlornly wandered away.

There seems to be no doubt that these animals feel grief as we do. They are also able to pass on learning and information from one individual and one generation to another. He watched the young ones in the herds he was studying learning to be wary and suspicious of his car. And he cites the example of a small South African park, where it was decided to eliminate a herd of 140 elephants, due to damage to citrus orchards. A single hunter took on the job of shooting one elephant at a time. Each time, the remainder of the herd grew more suspicious and aggressive, finally becoming entirely nocturnal and hiding in the densest thickets. It became impossible to shoot the last 30 individuals, for if the hunter pursued them into the forest, they turned on him, trying to trample him to death. Finally a sanctuary was given to the elephants, with a fence to keep them away from the farms. This happened in 1930, but even today, when the elephants that experienced this persecution are mostly dead, their offspring retain an acute fear and hatred of humans. They are still nocturnal and are considered the most dangerous elephants in Africa.

The fate of the African elephant is still hanging in the balance. There are parks all over the continent where they are protected, but poaching for ivory still goes on at an alarming rate. The demand for more farming lands in the developing Black nations is always growing and the habitat for wildlife is constantly shrinking. Whether these re-markable animals, so similar to humans in their large brains, their life spans, and their family social structure, will be allowed to live out this century is a matter of some doubt.

Our Nonhuman Cousins

The apes are our closest relatives in the animal world. So it is surprising to find that they live only about a third of our life span. Dr. Comfort says that only a few mammals can approach the elephant's 60 to 70 years. The rhino, the hippopotamus, and the ass all occasionally approach 50. But where are the apes? The gorilla has a span of about 34 years; the chimpanzee, 39; the gibbon and the orangutan, 32 plus.

How did our nearest relatives get left so far behind? For in some cases, they are as large as we are, or larger; and much stronger. We excel in only one thing: the brain. The human brain is the most complicated one in the animal kingdom, so perhaps the biological clock that regulates the life span is indeed located there. But then how can we account for the remarkably long lives of tortoises and birds with their small brains?

The great apes were unknown to the ancient civilizations. Although "apes" are mentioned in the Bible and appear in Egyptian paintings, the animal was probably the Barbary ape, a species of monkey and not an ape at all. Hanno, a Carthaginian explorer, sailed down the west coast of Africa in the fifth century B.C. and reported finding an island "full of savage people." From Hanno's description, these were probably chimpanzees, but Hanno believed them to be an unknown human race; and that is the nearest the ancient world came to knowing the great apes. Aristotle divided the monkeys into three groups: the Barbary apes, which are almost tailless; monkeys with tails; and dog-headed baboons. It was not until the great explorations of the sixteenth to eighteen centuries that rumors of human-like apes filtered into Europe, and it was not until 1738 that the first live chimpanzee was brought to England. The gorilla had to wait until the mid-nineteenth century to be discovered by the western world, and the mountain gorilla was not known there until 1902.

Because of this, there was great confusion about the different species of apes and how they should be classified and named. There was also confusion about the true nature of the creatures. Because of its great size, the gorilla was presumed to be a ferocious, frightening monster, and many tales were brought back from Africa about its horrendous behavior. It was not until the advent of the new science of ethology, in which scientists study animal behavior in the wild, that the gorilla was found to be a gentle, peace-loving creature. Like that other huge herbivore, the elephant, the gorilla is aroused to aggressive action only when it is attacked. And even then it is more apt to run away than to stay and fight.

The Biggest Apes

Gorillas are the most social of the apes. They live in groups usually comprising one or two old silver-backed males, several younger black-backed males, several females, and all their children of various ages. Usually there is one silver-backed male who is the leader and the others give way to him. He decides where the group will go within its forest range, when they will stop to rest, where they will spend the night. The others follow along. There is no defending of territories, as with so many other mammals. There is no fighting between males for the favors of a female. If two groups of gorillas meet in their wanderings, they may join for a while, feeding in the same area. Or they may pass each other, each group going in the opposite direction without incident. Occasionally one or more animals may change from one group to another.

Dr. George Schaller, who did the first modern study of the gorilla, only once saw anything approaching a fight between two big males. Each was leading a group and for some reason a disagreement flared. Each male put on the usual gorilla display of aggression. They roared. They pounded their chests. They chewed leaves and threw branches about. Finally they ended with their faces a few inches from each other, each trying to stare the other down. While all this went on, the other gorillas calmly continued to eat. No blows were struck. Nobody was clawed or bitten. When neither animal would back down, they simply separated, each male leading his group in a different direction.

Gorillas live in central Africa, in thick jungle or deep forest. When they are small, they do a lot of climbing in the trees. But the males especially get so heavy when they are grown that they live mostly on the ground. Nests are made on the ground by adults, both for sleeping and for resting during the day. Juveniles and females often build nests in trees, and in certain areas the males too climb into the trees to sleep.

The food of the gorilla seems to be entirely vegetarian. They eat leaves, vines, roots, bark, and fruit, all collected on the ground. They are never seen to drink and apparently get enough water in their food. No food-sharing has been observed as in other primates, and no use of tools.

The gorillas walk chiefly on their four legs, using the knuckles of the hand as a foot. Occasionally they stand up and walk for a short distance on two feet. They don't swing through the trees as the smaller primates and the monkeys do. They are quiet animals, never chorusing and shouting. Dian Fossey, who studied them for several years, records three types of sounds used for communication.

There is a close relationship between a gorilla mother and its young.   SAN DIEGO ZOO

One is a kind of belch, usually used when feeding and showing contentment. Another is what she called a pig grunt, a harsh exclamation often used by the leader to enforce discipline. Finally, there is a whooping bark which expresses alarm and alerts other members of the group to danger.

Young gorillas stay close to the mother until they are about three years old. They are the most helpless of the apes at birth, and the mother must hold the baby in her arms for about a month. After that it is strong enough to hold onto her by itself. At about three months it can ride on her back, and by five to six months can walk and climb alone. Some young gorillas become very attached to females other than their mothers. This is also true of chimpanzees.

The Almost Human Apes

Chimpanzees (*Pan troglodytes*) are considerably smaller than gorillas, but when adult they are stronger than humans and can be dangerous on occasion. Blood studies indicate that they are the most closely related to us of all the great apes. Chimpanzees have very large ears, while gorillas have small ones. This may relate to the fact that the chimps are noisy and often given to shouting and yelling as a group, an action known as chorusing. This can be heard for great distances and is probably a way of letting other chimps know where they are. Chimpanzees are the most communicative of the apes. In addition to chorusing, they drum on tree roots or logs, hoot loudly, and throw sticks and other things. Observers have heard them

Chimpanzees, shown here at play, communicate fully with each other and love to do things in a group.

scream, whine, snarl, bark, and mutter. Dr. Jane Goodall, who has studied chimpanzees extensively, notes what she calls the "pant-hoot" sound, given by a chimpanzee when rushing up to another group or to a new food source. She believes the animals identify each other by these sounds. She has also described the gestures that chimpanzees use to communicate with each other, many of which seem very human.

These apes do not keep to large groups as do the gorillas, nor do they have human-style families. There is no fighting between groups or individuals over territory. Mothers with infants will often stay together, thus forming a kind of nursery group. The mothers with their babies stay pretty much in one place and move about slowly. But the males range far afield, often in small groups, whose membership changes as one individual leaves the group and another joins it. Chimpanzees eat a lot of fruit, and these groups of exploring males signal the discovery of a good tree with ripe fruit so that others may come and enjoy it. When the seasons change from dry to wet, the animals often move over a wide range to find food.

Chimpanzees also eat meat. Dr. Goodall was the first to find them preying on smaller creatures, such as monkeys and the young of bush pigs. She also discovered that they make tools for various uses. She observed them using sticks and grasses to poke into termite nests. When they pulled out these "tools," they ate the termites that were clinging to them. If the piece of grass was not quite right, they would put it into their mouths to make a better point. These apes also crush leaves into a kind of sponge to sop up water for drinking. Most apes have an odd drinking habit. Because of their diet of fruit and leaves they do not seem to need as much water as other animals, and do not lap it up from a pool or river. But they have been seen to put their hands in the water and then with a small amount of liquid in the palm, they hold the hand over their head and let the water run down their fingers and drip into their mouths.

Chimps also use sticks and stones as missiles and weapons. They will throw things at intruders and have been seen to use a stick to attack a snake. However, they have few predators, the worst being humans. If left alone, they lead happy lives in their forest home. Only the leopard and occasionally the lion is a danger there and they do not seem to fear them especially. Scientists have made experiments with stuffed leopards, leaving the prop where the chimps would find it, and the animals immediately attacked it, beating it with a stick. Some observers believe the big cats may be wary of chimpanzees and are frightened off by the noise they make.

Scientists are confronted by a mystery in the chimpanzee. It is one of the most adaptable of all creatures and has developed skills and the use of tools while living in an environment that seems to make few demands on it. This is at variance with the scientific theory that skills are evolved when the environment demands them. It is believed that our distant ancestors, the first ape-humans, left the forest and moved out into the plains in search of better food sources. And in order to catch and eat the animals of the plains, they had to develop the use of tools. But here are the chimpanzees, living in a forest environment, using tools and primitive weapons. One suggested theory is that the ancestors of the chimpanzees may also have moved out onto the plains but that those early ape-humans drove them back into the forest habitat. However, this is still in the realm of speculation.

Close to Extinction

The two smaller species of apes live in southeast Asia. Probably because they are smaller and inhabit tropical rain forests they are all arboreal. That is, they swing through the trees and when escaping, take to the tree-tops instead of running on the ground. The orangutan (*Pongo pygmaeus*) is the only unsocial ape and it is the one closest to extinction. While it may once have lived in much of southeast Asia, it is now found only in small areas on the islands of Sumatra and Borneo.

The orang is almost as large as the chimpanzee; an adult male may weigh 91 kilograms (about 200 pounds) and thus it is no such swift arborealist as the gibbon. It moves slowly through the trees, not much faster than three miles an hour, making it fairly easy for an observer to keep up with it, and also making it easy for a hunter to shoot or capture the creatures. George Schaller found that orangs in Sarawak were very fond of fruit growing in swamp areas. He suggests that this must encourage their staying in the trees, since movement along such ground would be difficult.

Like the gorilla, orangs have relatively small ears and are quiet animals, never indulging in the noisy chorusing of the chimpanzees. Their communicative sounds seem

The orangutan is quiet and rather slow-moving. It is the only nonsocial kind of ape. This fact seems to be borne out by its expression here, though we must be careful not to mistake facial structure for a show of attitude or assume that ape expressions necessarily mean the same as ours.

to be confined to lip-smacking, belching, the squeal of an infant, and very rarely a roar from an adult male.

Orangs get up late, around 8:00 A.M., from a tree nest constructed the night before. Occasionally an individual will not leave its nest until noon, and they all make new nests and retire for the night by 6:30 P.M., thus spending 60 per cent of the day resting. An unusual activity observed in orangs is the making of a shelter against rain. The orang builds this as it would for a nest, but it is constructed from underneath and the animal sits under it.

The only stable group attachment is that of mother and child. One observer, Peter S. Rodman, watched a female orang who was carrying a small male of about a year. She was followed by her six-year-old daughter, an adolescent that would soon leave the little group. During the year that Rodman observed these animals, the young female gradually wandered farther and farther from her mother, toward the end often spending the nights alone.

The infant clung to his mother's hair, occasionally suckling or taking food from her mouth. She paid little attention to him as she fed. Only once did Rodman see her kiss his head and a few times groom his fur. Sometimes the baby would leave her and climb along a branch or build a play nest. When the mother went for a long walk through the trees, the baby rode on her back.

One evening the scientist heard a male orangutan roaring from across the river, and saw the female and the two offspring come down to the river's edge. He knew that in time the mother would have a new infant, the daughter would have left the group, and the little male would be pushed out of the nest. This action is always accompanied

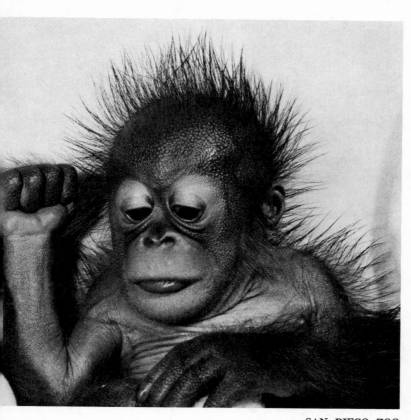

It is only toward an infant that a mother orangutan shows a strong attachment.

by screaming tantrums on the part of the ejected child, which can be heard for a distance throughout the forest.

The orangutan population has been depleted to such an extent that the governments of Borneo and Sumatra have made laws protecting them. But because of the spread of logging and agriculture, their habitat is constantly shrinking. Poaching is also hard to control. The mothers are shot so that the young may be captured and sold to zoos.

The Gibbon

Gibbons (*Hylobates lar*) have a much wider range and distribution than orangutans. They also inhabit southeast Asia, including much of the mainland and some adjacent islands. They are considerably smaller than the other apes, being more the size of a large monkey, and are entirely tree-dwellers. There are several species of gibbon spread throughout this territory.

These apes have large ears, like the chimpanzees, and like those apes, they are very noisy. They indulge in group chorusing, apparently to communicate with each other over distances. Since they seem to be territorial, the cries may warn other groups away. For gibbons are social animals, going about in family-sized groups. Usually such groups consist of an adult male and female and several young of different ages. Scientists refer to this as a "typical monogamous family," and the gibbons are the only apes in which this behavior holds true.

They are also the only ape species in which male and female are the same size. In all the others, the males are much larger and take precedence over the females in the social order. Gibbon females might be said to be emancipated. They are not ordered around by their mates.

Since gibbons are so small, they can sleep safely in the crotch of a tree, and therefore they make no nests. Their food is entirely vegetarian, being mostly fruits with a scattering of leaves and flowers thrown in. Their principal way of traveling is from branch to branch, swinging by their long arms through the trees with remarkable ease and agility. When they are alarmed, they may leap 20 feet from tree to tree. But usually they move at a leisurely pace.

If two groups meet, they may intermingle for a while, and observers surmise that at such times new groups may be formed, the excess older children going off with each other. But normally each group has its special territory, varying from 16 to 100 hectares (about 40 to 250 acres). The family spends the night in the center of its territory, and every morning the apes call and chorus from the tops of their trees, warning other gibbons away. If they notice another group trespassing, they rush to the spot, where the two groups confront each other, barking and throwing sticks and shaking branches in a determined effort to make the others back down. These displays of aggression seem to be sufficient to settle the matter of ownership, and they are mostly performed by the adult males. For this reason the males spend an hour longer in feeding than do the females, making up for time lost in defending the territory.

Gibbons live a fortunate life in a habitat with plenty of food and no predators; probably most of them reach their approximate 30-year life span. They have not been extensively hunted by humans because many of the peoples in those regions consider the gibbons to be sacred and the reincarnation of their ancestors. Nevertheless, at the rate that humankind is expanding, it will only be a matter of time before their habitat is usurped. So, even though individuals are not in much danger, gibbons as a species are.

Conservationists today fear that the great apes will not be with us for much longer. Efforts are being made to save them, but the wild orang will probably disappear before this century is ended. The gorillas may live into the twenty-first century, if they are lucky. The chimpanzee should do better and survive into the middle of the next century, and the gibbon should be with us somewhat longer, but not very much.

6

Trees to a Ripe Old Age

The tissues of animals are not the only kinds of living tissue that can keep alive for long spans. We are used to the idea of annual flowering plants that are finished in a year, and perennials that live successfully for decades in gardens and parks. These are not especially impressive. But trees can surprise us, for certain kinds have astonishingly long spans. And some plants in their embryo form—seeds—have done even better.

At one time, Australia claimed to have the oldest living tree. It was a macrozamia, said to be between 10,000 and 15,000 years old. This is a good example of how gross exaggeration can creep into claims of great age.

The macrozamia tree is a cycad, an ancient form of vegetation going back to the Mesozoic era, when the reptiles ruled, about 200 million to 60 million years ago. Cycads are plants of a fernlike or palmlike appearance. Male and female "flowers" grow on different plants. They are considered to be halfway between ferns and true flowering plants, and thus are the most primitive of all seed-bearers. The seeds of some cycads provide food for the aborigines. But they are poisonous in their natural state, and after being ground into flour, must be washed in running water for 24 hours before it can be cooked and eaten.

There are three genera of cycads in Australia, one being the macrozamia tree, found only on that continent. A large specimen of *Macrozamia denisonii* grew in Queensland on Tamborine Mountain, southeast of Brisbane. It was 20 feet high and believed to be very old. It is hard to judge the age of cycads, as it must be done from their leaf scars, and in older specimens the scars become obscured. However, Professor C. J. Chamberlain, the world authority on

A female Cycas media, one of the cycads, in fruit. They are the most primitive kinds of seed-bearing plants in existence.

AUSTRALIAN INFORMATION SERVICE

cycads, studied the tree and decided that it must be between 1000 and 1500 years old. But when these data were cabled to the world press, an extra zero was inadvertently added to the figures. Thus, for some years it was believed that a tree existed in Australia that had lived for ten millennia.

The ancient tree on Tamborine Mountain was known as Grandfather Peter to the white settlers. It was cut down by vandals sometime around 1930. Unfortunately, this tragedy was not immediately discovered, and when scientists tried to replant the top, they were unsuccessful because decay had set in.

The Aged Sequoias

In America we have several species of trees that are known to have lived at least twice as long as Australia's macrozamia, and even more in some cases. There are two species of the genus Sequoia, both of which are found in California. *Sequoia gigantea* grows at an altitude of 4500 to 8000 feet on the western slopes of the Sierra Nevada; *S. sempervirens* is found in the fog belt along the coast, a few groves extending up into Oregon.

The Big Trees, as *S. gigantea* are popularly known, were discovered in 1852 by a miner who was hunting a bear. When the man saw the trees, he was so impressed that he forgot about the bear and hastened to bring his friends to see this wonder. Since then parks and sanctuaries have been created to preserve the trees, and names have been given to some of the biggest.

It is difficult to say which is the larger of the two

species, for while the coast redwoods reach staggering heights, the Big Trees have larger trunks and a greater spread. They grow in groves, often widely separated. Perhaps this is because the seed wings are narrow and never fall far from the parent tree. But little squirrels run about in the branches and cut down the cones, carrying them away to bury in their winter caches.

The sequoias stand normally from 76 to 85 meters (about 250 to 280 feet) tall, but unusually tall ones may reach 91 to 106 meters (about 300 to 350 feet). Their trunks may be anywhere from 12 to 27 feet in diameter. It is said that one fallen, hollow giant was so big that a man could ride his horse through it without ducking his head. Such trunks may lie for hundreds of years without decaying. In fact, the wood of the sequoias is so durable that it is much prized for many purposes, from house-building to making souvenirs. This has caused extensive lumbering and we are fortunate that many of the groves are now protected in national parks. Otherwise these ancient giants might soon be eradicated from the earth.

The coast redwoods are just as impressive as the mighty *gigantea*. A walk among these towering trees is like a visit to a cathedral. And it is awe-inspiring to realize that many of them were growing at the time of the birth of Christ. Since the science of counting and interpreting tree rings,

This is the General Grant Tree in the Kings Canyon National Park in California. This huge sequoia is the world's second-largest living tree. Note the two people standing below. NATIONAL PARK SERVICE

called dendrochronology, has been developed, it has been found that many of the trees are from 1800 to 2500 years old, with exceptional giants approaching 4000 years.

Scientists have wondered why these trees have such a long life span. One answer may be the large amount of tannic acid found in the sap. This is a chemical used in fire extinguishers, and it seems to have made the great trees very fire-resistant. Even after the major part of the tree has been burned, it can rejuvenate itself and continue growing. One can stand inside the hollow shell of a burned-out tree and look upward hundreds of feet to where the green leaves are still growing. Sequoias also have very thick bark, once they have gotten past the juvenile stage: 30 to 61 centimeters (about one to two feet) thick in *gigantea;* eight to 30 centimeters (about three inches to one foot) in *sempervirens.*

Even when a redwood is cut down, the roots can still send out new shoots, and a fallen log can start new life, so that sometimes there is a whole row of little trees springing up from the fallen giant, or clustered around an old stump. Once sequoias grew all over the world, but now they are found only in this small area of our western states. They are a treasure from the past, well worth saving and studying.

The Dramatic Bristlecone Pines

For some time it was thought that the redwoods were the oldest living things in the world. But when scientists began to study the situation, they found that there is another tree growing in our western states which is even

The very rugged bristlecone pine can live as long as 5000 years.

older. This is the bristlecone pine (*Pinus aristata*). Specimens were found that could be dated by tree-ring count at around 5000 years. This was especially surprising, since the bristlecone grows in a far more hostile environment than that enjoyed by the sequoias.

The bristlecone is an alpine tree. It grows singly rather than in groves, at altitudes from 2286 to 3292 meters (about 7500 to 10,800 feet), on exposed sites in thin, dry, rocky soil. It is a midget compared to the redwoods, nine to 12 meters (about 30 to 40 feet) high and no more than 61 centimeters (about 2 feet) thick. Like the redwoods, it is an evergreen, having bushy needles and bristle-like prickles on the ends of its cone scales, from which it gets its name. It grows very slowly, reaching maturity after 200 or 250 years and then enduring for thousands.

And it survives through the harshest conditions. The fierce winds of these heights have blown most of the trees

The strong winds at high altitudes sometimes blow bristlecones into very strange shapes.

FRANCIS LIGHTNER

into grotesque shapes. The air is thin, the soil is sparse and dry. One wonders how anything at all can grow there, let alone persist for millennia. Even fire can be withstood by these ancient trees, for if most of the tree is burned and dead, a small vein of live tissue is all that is needed to keep the tree alive. Even the oldest trees still bring forth fertile seeds. Because of its twisted form, the wood has no commercial value and so it is not threatened by lumbering.

These trees are scattered through our western states, in Utah, Arizona, New Mexico, Colorado, and Nevada, as well as in the White Mountains of California. The same tragedy that overtook the ancient macrozamia in Australia was suffered by our oldest bristlecone, estimated to be 5000 years old. This famous tree was cut down in Nevada in 1964. For this reason, park wardens are reluctant to give out the exact locations of the oldest trees.

With the invention of the Swedish increment borer, it is now possible to take a core from a living tree without harming the tree. The bore extracted is no thicker than a pencil lead, so small that it can be inserted in a soda straw for transportation to the laboratory. There it is carefully smoothed out and stained with kerosene so that the rings are more definite. Then it is studied under the microscope. The tree soon fills in the bore hole with resin.

As the science of dendrochronology improved, it was found that patterns could be recognized in the rings that could be matched with those of other wood and other trees. A piece of driftwood could supply information. Soon a master calendar was put together so that every year could be counted back to 6200 B.C. This has proved useful to other scientific studies. Weather conditions can be analyzed and cycles mapped out from which we may be able to predict future weather. Pollen grains have been found trapped in ancient bark, making it possible to compare plants that grew in 1300 B.C. with those of 350 A.D.

But the most startling revelations of the bristlecone tree rings have been in the realm of prehistory. The tree-ring calendar has found errors in radio-carbon dating, probably because of fluctuations in the amount of carbon in the atmosphere. This has forced prehistorians to revise their ideas about Old World history. Many of the ancient tombs and structures of Europe and England turn out to be much older than hitherto believed. Stonehenge is now thought to be older than the pyramids. This puts many of the achievements of prehistoric Europe—metalworking as well as building—before their development in the Near East and negates the previous theory that those arts spread from there to Europe and the British Isles.

For more immediate efforts, these trees are helping check the amounts of air pollution from West Coast cars and industries and to record the effects of scientific efforts in weather control. Bristlecone pine wood is even used to monitor changes in the earth's magnetism. Thus these ancient trees, clinging precariously to the high mountains, are helping to increase our knowledge, while they never cease to cause wonder by their incredible survival.

Plants can extend their life spans enormously also as seeds. We know that seeds can be kept from a good harvest year and sown years later when needed, if they are preserved in the proper conditions. A cool, dry storage is required for most seeds; in northern areas, many seeds must go through winter temperatures to germinate successfully the following spring. On the other hand, the seeds of some pines require a forest fire to burst their shells and start germination, thus reforesting areas that have been devastated.

In recent years it has been found that seeds from an ancient tomb in Argentina could still sprout and grow into plants. These were seeds of a herb, achira (*Canna sp.*). They were part of a necklace and had been placed inside a walnut shell to make a rattle. Bones found in the tomb have been dated by the carbon-14 method at 550 years.

Still older seeds that proved to be viable are those of the arctic tundra lupine (*Lupinus arcticus*), found in a lemming's burrow that was unearthed by mining operations in the Yukon Territory in 1954. The lemming had brought these seeds into its burrow during the Pleistocene Age, and the seeds and rodent bones are at least 10,000 years old. The seeds, when planted, developed into healthy lupine plants that brought forth flowers.

In a similar case, bacteria were recovered from cores brought up from several hundred feet below the Antarctic ice. Geologists believe the core material was on the surface of Antarctica between 10,000 and one million years ago. The bacteria remained frozen for that time, but when cultivated in the laboratory, they grew and developed, and most of them reproduced themselves. Bacteria are not plants (as they were formerly considered to be) but these members of the Monera showed dramatically the possibilities for fantastic life spans in at least some single cells.

7

We
Humans

The Bible tells us that our life span is "three score years and ten," or 70 years. Until the advent of modern medicine and the general improvement in living conditions, that seems to have been the usual limit for human life. It was very much the exception for anyone to live past that age, and the majority of people never even approached it. Life expectancy around 1880 was only 35 to 40 years for men and 37 to 42 for women. Put another way, less than 10 per cent of the people lived past the age of 70. Today, more than 50 per cent do so.

There are, however, a few limited areas in the world where old people are living far beyond the 100 mark. These include a village in Ecuador called Vilcabamba; an area in the Caucasus, in the Soviet Union, known as Abkhazia; and another region in the Himalayas, called Hunza. In all these places it has been found that there are oldsters who count their years anywhere from 100 to 130 and occasionally higher. What is more, they are active people who do not seem to suffer from the usual infirmities of old age.

Since these facts have been brought to the attention

of the scientific world, doctors and other specialists have gone to the areas to study the situation and try to learn the reasons for this remarkable longevity. Early in the 1970s, Dr. Alexander Leaf, of the Massachusetts General Hospital and the Harvard University Medical School, made long and difficult journeys to these remote regions to study the people and learn what is fact and what is fiction about them.

All three sites are in mountainous areas, remote from the world at large, where the people live an agricultural way of life in a rugged but unpolluted environment. Here old people continue to pursue an active life, helping with the farm labor and housework to the best of their ability. They are always surrounded by family and friends, and are given great respect because of their wisdom and experience gathered over many years.

Clean Air, No Mosquitoes

Vilcabamba, in Ecuador's Loja Province, is in a valley over a mile high, surrounded by towering mountains. The ancient Incans called it "the sacred valley." Even then it was considered a good place to live. The town was settled by Spaniards in the seventeenth century and is still a small, primitive village with houses of wood and adobe clustered around a square. The crisp, clear mountain air discourages the noxious animal life of the surrounding jungle. There are no snakes, spiders, or even mosquitoes. Clear mountain streams provide pure water for drinking and bathing.

Because the inhabitants are Roman Catholics, there are

baptismal records that make it possible to check the claims of longevity. Active residents of 123 and 142 years are seen working in their gardens, and there are many people in their eighties and nineties still active in farm work. The visiting doctors could find none of the diseases of old age among them, and report that death usually comes from an accident or from influenza, brought in by some tourist.

Scientists were naturally interested in the diet of these people, and found it to be quite frugal: soup made from grain and corn; beans and potatoes. They also have oranges, bananas and vegetables, but only about one ounce of meat a week. There is little fat in the diet, and what milk is available is made into cheese. The average caloric intake is only 1200 calories a day. Protein and fat come mostly from vegetables. No fat people were found in Vilcabamba. However, almost everybody smoked tobacco and enjoyed a daily ration of brandy and a special Ecuadorian liquor made from sugar cane. One of the possible reasons noted for the longevity of the Vilcabambans was the peace and tranquility of the place. There is none of the hurry, confusion, and tension of our industrial civilization.

The people of Hunza, called Hunzukuts, have a diet remarkably like that of the Vilcabambans. This little realm, with a population of 40,000, lies in a remote and inaccessible region of the Himalayas, so isolated that their language, called Burushaski, is related to no other language in the world. There is no written language and hence no records, making it difficult for investigators to verify claims of great age. The ruler of Hunza, called the

Mir, sometimes helped to check age claims, as he knew the history of the state. But although these claims may be less accurate than some, Dr. Leaf says that he spoke with a number of very old and very fit people.

One Hunzukut, whom the doctor wanted to interview, was tending his goats in the high alpine pastures. Kosta Kashig, who claimed to be 106, regularly spent the summer at 6000 feet in the mountains, so Dr. Leaf set out in the early morning to climb there. The way was so rugged that two of his companions—one being the interpreter—gave up and went back, and it was only with the greatest effort that the scientist completed the climb. He suspected that his subject might be 90 rather than 106 years, but his ability to scramble over the mountain trails in pursuit of his goats was amazing.

Just as in Vilcabamba, the very old are held in high regard in Hunza. This is exemplified by the fact that the Mir's advisory council is made up of the oldest people in his realm. Every morning when court opens, the council of 20 elders sits on a circle of carpets at the foot of the Mir's throne. They listen to disputes among the citizens and then discuss the problems. Their discussion and advice help the ruler to dispense justice.

Is It Diet?

The sparse, low-calorie diets of the people of Vilcabamba and Hunza fit in well with modern medical theories of how to prevent such illnesses as arthritis and heart disease. But when Dr. Leaf visited the centenarians in the Caucasus region, his confidence in those theories was somewhat shaken. Abkhazia, a region in the Georgian Republic of the Soviet Union, borders the Black Sea and nestles in the foothills of the Caucasus mountains. The people here are farmers and shepherds, as in the other two regions, but the standard of living is higher. Better land for farming and grazing makes the difference, and the old people eat more (1700 to 1900 calories) and more meat is available. Milk and cheese are eaten at all meals. In addition, many of the people interviewed begin the day with a glass of vodka, and homemade wine is served at other meals. Cigarettes are freely enjoyed. The oldest person whom Dr. Leaf talked to was Mrs. Lasuria, a woman of 130. Only two years earlier she had been persuaded to give up her job as a tea picker. She admitted to smoking a pack of cigarettes a day, a practice frowned on by doctors in this country.

Is It Moderation?

In Abkhazia there are no words in the language for "old people." Citizens who have passed the mark of 100 are called "long-living people." A census taken in 1954 found that 2.58 per cent of the population was over 90. In the United States, only 0.4 per cent have passed that age. When questioned about the number of healthy, active old people, the Abkhazians said it is due to moderate habits in work, diet, and sex. The usual age for marriage is around 30. It may be significant that almost all the "long-living people" are or have been married. One man in his hundredth year had recently married his seventh wife. He said, "My first six wives were all wonderful

Gerontologists—scientists who specialize in aging—think that frequent moderate exercise helps to keep humans living longer.

women, but this present wife is an angry woman, and I have aged at least ten years since marrying her. If a man has a good and kind wife, he can easily live 100 years."

There are at least ten different ethnic groups in Abkhazia. Unlike the remote valleys of Vilcabamba and Hunza, it extends from the seacoast to the mountainous areas, 914 to 1371 meters (about 3000 to 4500 feet) high. From childhood on, all the citizens work at some farming task. There is no such thing as retirement. Even the centenarians lead active, productive lives. This constant, moderate exercise may have a bearing on the problem. It was found to be common to all three localities. But the restricted, fat-free diet, common to Hunza and Vilcabamba was not so evident in Abkhazia, and there appeared to be more centenarians there than in the other two areas.

Dr. Leaf says that there is still the genetic factor. In most cases, the old people had had long-lived parents or siblings. And in these remote villages there was little inclination to marry an outsider. Thus the same genes persisted from generation to generation. So far as is known, there is no gene for longevity. But there can be an absence of bad genes: those that make us subject to fatal or crippling diseases, such as heart attacks or arthritis.

What's the Answer?

Whatever the explanation may be for the remarkable longevity of people in these three regions, specialists in aging are studying them, hoping to find answers that may be of benefit to all humanity. There are many possibilities for providing part of the answer, among them the effect, if any, of stronger ultraviolet light or other radiations from space at the higher altitudes, or of breathing thinner air.

While scientists are studying human longevity in the field, work is also going on in laboratories all over the world, attacking the problem from different angles. Many investigators are hopeful that they may soon unravel the mysteries of the so-called "clock of aging," which is believed to control genetically the rate and age at which each individual will age and die. Such knowledge would advance medical science immeasurably and help to control and possibly cure the diseases of old age. Among the many researchers at work on the problem, there are two outstanding scientists with opposing views.

Dr. Leonard Hayflick, formerly of Stanford University, believes that the answer must be found in the nucleus of the cell. He has kept human cells alive in culture and watched them divide. He found that after about 50 divisions, this activity would cease and the cells would reach a point that he calls "Phase III." After that, the cells died. In a number of experiments, Hayflick put cells in a deep-freeze of liquid nitrogen. The cell cultures were all at different stages of development, but when they were thawed out and brought back to normal living conditions over a period of years, each cell "remembered" where it had left off growing and continued to divide the requisite number of times until it reached Phase III; then it died.

Other experimenters in this line of inquiry have found that cells taken from young people live longer in the laboratory and go through more divisions, whereas those taken from older people have fewer divisions to make before

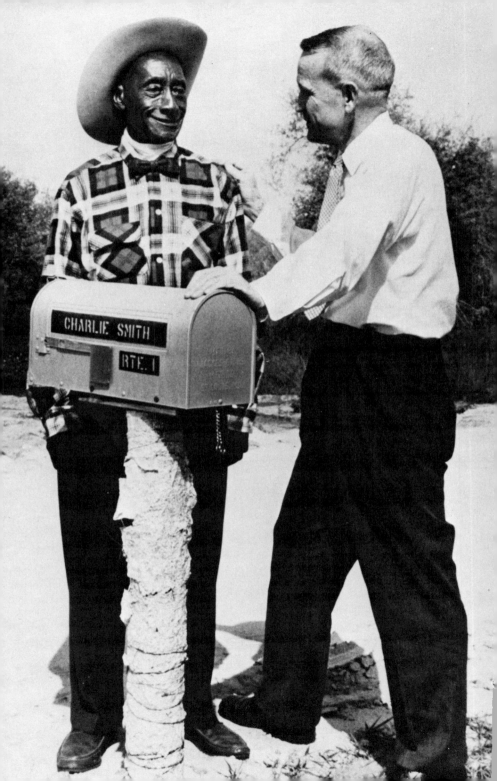

they reach Phase III. Cells taken from very old individuals still make a few divisions in the laboratory before reaching Hayflick's limit, a fact which implies that few people live out their potential life spans.

In other significant experiments it was found that if the nucleus of a young cell, having many potential divisions left, was removed and substituted for the nucleus of an old cell that had almost reached Phase III, the old cell was seemingly rejuvenated, and went on to complete all the divisions that would have been made by the young cell. Similarly, if the nucleus of an old cell, with only a dozen divisions left, was inserted in a young cell, that cell would make only a dozen divisions before reaching Phase III. These experiments convinced Hayflick that it must be the DNA in the chromosomes of the nucleus that control the "clock of aging."

An opposing view is taken by the gerontologist Dr. W. Donner Denckla, formerly of the Roche Institute of Molecular Biology and now at the Harvard Medical School. Denckla believes that the "clock of aging" is located in the brain and is governed by the glands and hormones. He says, "I don't care what happens to cells in tissue culture. What is important is what people die of." Since cells in tissue culture are beyond normal hormonal influence,

Charlie Smith, left, the oldest social security beneficiary in the United States and perhaps the oldest man in the country, was born on July 4, 1842. Modern research on aging may perhaps make ages of 100 or more rather common in the future. HEW

he feels that they are unrelated to what goes on in the human body. His theory is that a "death hormone" is released into the body at scheduled times.

Denckla believes that the thyroid gland, which is controlled by the pituitary, is the chief factor in aging. In his laboratory he was able to extract material from the pituitary glands of rats. This substance, refined, he calls DECO, from "decreasing consumption of oxygen." He believes that the pituitary releases this material into the bloodstream and that it hampers the work of the thyroid gland, which is all-important to the proper functioning of the animal system. In his laboratory he has been able to rejuvenate old rats by removing their pituitary glands (believed to be secreting DECO, the agent of aging) and administering thyroxine (the product of the thyroid gland). If he gave thyroxine to the aging rats while they still had their pituitary glands, nothing was achieved, because the DECO secreted by the pituitary was inhibiting the cells from using the thyroxine.

These two approaches to the problem of aging seem to be diametrically opposed. But as more work is done and more secrets are discovered, they may be found to complement each other. Many people believe that in the not-too-distant future there may be a major breakthrough in such research and that some of these questions will be answered. When that happens, we can look forward to the control of many of the diseases that afflict people, such as cancer, heart trouble, and arthritis. We can look forward to longer and healthier lives.

Glossary

alpine   A high mountainous region, like the Alps

arboreal   Living in or among trees

brachiation   Swinging from branch to branch among the trees

castrate   To remove the male sex organs

centenarian   A person 100 years old or older

chromosome   The part of a cell that carries the genes and determines heredity

copulation   Sexual union

cryptobiosis   A state of suspended animation in which some of the lower animals can survive conditions that would normally kill them

cuticle   A skin or covering

dendrochronology   The science of measuring time from tree rings

estrogen   The female hormone

ethology   The study of animal behavior

genetics   The study and processes of heredity

germinate   To start to grow; to sprout

gestation period   The time that the young mammal spends in its mother's womb

habitat   The area where an animal lives or a plant grows

hibernation   Passing the winter in a state of sleep and low metabolic activity *hormones* Chemicals given off by a gland, which stimulate various bodily organs and systems

Hymenoptera A group of social insects which includes bees, wasps, ants, and termites

incubate To sit on eggs or otherwise warm them sufficiently to hatch them

inhibit To check or restrain some activity

invertebrate An animal without a backbone

lichens A group of plants growing on rocks. Each lichen is made up of a fungus and an alga which grow harmoniously together.

metabolism The way in which an animal or plant makes energy from its food

metamorphosis A marked, rather abrupt change in form that a creature goes through in growing from infant to adult

methuselah A very long-lived creature. From the biblical patriarch Methuselah, said to have lived 969 years.

migration A periodic movement of some animals from one region to another, usually with the seasons

monogamous Having only one mate

neoteny The holding over of juvenile characteristics into the adult stage

nocturnal Active at night

noxious Harmful or unhealthy

ovipositor A special part of a female insect, used for depositing eggs. It has a sharp point that can penetrate leaves, stems and the bark of trees.

parthenogenesis Reproduction by virgin females in which the egg develops without fertilization by the male

redirected aggression A situation in which animosity is felt for one person or object but the attack is made on another

regurgitation The bringing up of undigested food; a method used by some birds and mammals when feeding their young

rejuvenate To make young again

senescence Old age, or growing old

termitarium   A nest built by termites
testosterone   The male hormone
torpidity   Sleepiness, as in a hibernating animal
toxic   Poisonous
vertebrate   An animal with a backbone
viable   Born alive and capable of living

Suggested Reading

Books

Harold L. Babcock, *Turtles of the Northeastern United States* (Dover, N.Y., 1971)

Arthur Cleveland Bent, *Life Histories of North American Cuckoos, Goatsuckers, Hummingbirds and Their Allies,* Part II (Dover, N.Y., 1964)

Alex Comfort, *Ageing: The Biology of Senescence* (Holt, N.Y., 1964)

Mary C. Dickerson, *The Frog Book* (Dover, N.Y., 1969)

Iain and Oria Douglas-Hamilton, *Among The Elephants* (Viking, N.Y., 1975)

Anne Dunbar Graham, *A Bird in My Bed* (Taplinger, N.Y., 1971)

Ian McMillan, *Man and the California Condor* (Dutton, N.Y., 1968)

Donald Culross Peattie, *A Natural History of Western Trees* (Houghton Mifflin, Boston, 1953)

Vernon Reynolds, *The Apes* (Dutton, N.Y., 1967)

Ivan T. Sanderson, *The Dynasty of Abu* (Knopf, N.Y., 1962)

Jack Denton Scott, *Speaking Wildly* (Morrow, N.Y., 1966)

George Gaylord Simpson, *Penguins* (Yale University Press, New Haven, Ct., 1976)

H. Rucker Smyth, *Amphibians and Their Ways* (Macmillan, N.Y., 1962)

Ian Thornton, *Darwin's Islands* (Natural History Press, N.Y., 1971)

Jane van Lawick-Goodall, *My Friends, The Wild Chimpanzees* (National Geographic Society, Washington, D.C., 1967)

Ruth Winter, *Ageless Aging* (Crown, N.Y., 1973)

Magazine Articles

David Cohen, "The Meaning of Ageing," *New Scientist* (London), Mar. 21, 1974

Alex Comfort, "The Causes of Ageing," *Science Journal* (London), March 1965

David Davies, "A Shangri-la in Ecuador," *New Scientist* (London), Feb. 1, 1973

Lee Ehrman and W. Strickberger Monroe, "Flies Mating," *Natural History*, Nov. 1960

Dian Fossey, "More Years with Mountain Gorillas," *National Geographic*, Oct. 1971

Stephen Jay Gould, "Our Allotted Lifetimes," *Natural History*, Aug.–Sept. 1977

———, "The 120-year Bamboo Clock," *Natural History*, April 1977

Leonard Hayflick, "The Biology of Aging," *Natural History*, Aug.–Sept. 1977

Weldon F. Heald, "Methuselah of Trees: The Bristlecone Pine," *Audubon Magazine*, Jan.–Feb. 1964

Alice Hopf, "A Crucial M-Day for the Monarch," *Audubon*, Sept.–Oct. 1962

Darwin Lambert, "What the Ancient Pines Teach Us," *Reader's Digest*, Dec. 1972

Alexander Leaf, M.D., "Search for the Oldest People," *National Geographic*, Jan. 1973

Irene McManus, "The Story of the Bristlecones," *American Forests*, March 1973

Lorus and Margery Milne, "On Estimating Ages," *Natural History*, April 1958

Diane R. Nelson, "The Hundred-Year Hibernation of the Water Bear," *Natural History,* Aug.–Sept. 1975

Raymond G. Pierce, "Programing the Insect's Life Cycle," *The Science Teacher,* April 1969

Colin Renfrew, "Carbon 14 and the Prehistory of Europe," *Scientific American,* Oct. 1971

Albert Rosenfeld, "Are We Programmed to Die?" *Saturday Review,* Oct. 2, 1976

Rudolf and Marvin J. Schmid, "Living Links with the Past," *Natural History,* March 1975

Bernard L. Strehler, "A New Age for Aging," *Natural History,* Feb. 1973

Janet Bascom Sutter, "The Oldest Tree in the World," *Home Garden and Flower Grower,* March 1972

Jane van Lawick-Goodall, "Tool-Using Bird," *National Geographic,* May 1968

David P. Willoughby, "Animal Ages," *Natural History,* Dec. 1969

Index